Essays on Style and Language

Linguistic and Critical Approaches to Literary Style

Edited by
Roger G. Fowler

Routledge Revivals
Routledge
Taylor & Francis Group

First published in 1966
by Routledge and Kegan Paul

This edition first published in 2018 by Routledge
2 Park Square, Milton Park, Abingdon, Oxon, OX14 4RN
and by Routledge
711 Third Avenue, New York, NY 10017

Routledge is an imprint of the Taylor & Francis Group, an informa business

Publisher's Note
The publisher has gone to great lengths to ensure the quality of this reprint but points out that some imperfections in the original copies may be apparent.

Disclaimer
The publisher has made every effort to trace copyright holders and welcomes correspondence from those they have been unable to contact.
A Library of Congress record exists under ISBN: 66070850

ISBN 13: 978-1-138-56399-5 (hbk)
ISBN 13: 978-1-315-12221-2 (ebk)
ISBN 13: 978-1-138-56409-1 (pbk)

Routledge Revivals

Essays on Style and Language

First published in 1966, this book is contributed to by authors who share an interest in the literary uses of language. The book gives a close analysis of the language of literature contributed to by critics and linguists, examining linguistic theory and poetry, and as part of this the rhythm and metre of English poetry is deconstructed. The middle chapters of the book address the interaction of linguistic dimensions, while two medievalist scholars conclude the volume. This book is suitable for students and scholars concerned with English literature and linguistics.

Essays on STYLE *and* LANGUAGE

Contributors

ROGER FOWLER

BRIAN LEE

ALLAN RODWAY

J. McH. SINCLAIR

P. J. WEXLER

A. L. BINNS

G. N. LEECH

J. NORTON-SMITH

R. F. LAWRENCE

Essays on

STYLE

and

LANGUAGE

Linguistic and Critical Approaches to Literary Style

Edited by

ROGER FOWLER

Routledge and Kegan Paul

LONDON

First published 1966
by Routledge & Kegan Paul Limited
Broadway House, 68–74 Carter Lane
London E.C.4

ISBN 0 7100 1391 4 (c)
ISBN 0 7100 6870 0 (p)

Contents

Preface

CHAPTER 6 of this book begins with a comment which is firmly impressed on the editor's consciousness: 'that the various authors believe they have something in common, and that, whatever this is, it is in some sense novel'. What they have in common is something sufficiently undogmatic to take the edge off any sweeping claim, but sufficiently positive and novel, it is hoped, to justify the collection of these essays and their publication.

They share an interest in the literary uses of language; in the development of methods and terms for describing them with precision; and in the consideration of the uses to which stylistic analysis in these terms can be put in a critical and historical study of literature. The book sprang from discussions among some of the linguistic contributors, who believed that it would be useful to explore in print, in both theoretical and practical ways, an area where linguistics and literary criticism overlap. Its novelty, therefore, consists partly in viewing literary style through the eyes of the modern linguist. Despite the uncertain standing of 'linguistic stylistics', evidence of interest in close analysis of the language of literature can be found in the writings of many critics and linguists in recent years. It was heartening for us to be joined quite quickly by a number of people outside linguistics who wished to contribute to an informal symposium.

We do not intend to prescribe an all-embracing programme for stylistics; nor to lay down definitions, nor specify particular methods of analysis, except in respect of particular kinds of texts. And although linguists and critics are both represented, this is not (as is Sebeok's *Style in Language*) a confrontation of camps. A range of attitudes and emphases is illustrated, and it is hoped that the distinction between linguist and critic is presented as one of the less prominent distinctions within this range. No attempt has been made to induce conformity in the details of approach in what is, after all, still a field for tentative exploration; so, for example, there is no standardization of linguistic terminology or analytic techniques.

The first two chapters, although not primarily organized around the history of linguistics and criticism, draw attention to some factors in the upsurge of reciprocal interest in the last few years, and explore some points of theory. Then Allan Rodway considers the application of analysis to the characterization of a 'period' style, incidentally touching on some critical questions of a more general nature. Chapters 4–6 form a group, despite the fact that their authors would, I am sure, find it difficult to write from a linguistic platform shared in all its details. The interest in all three is in the interaction of linguistic dimensions, especially in the interaction of grammar and metre to form 'grammetric' patterns, which are here studied in widely differing types of poetry. A. L. Binns revives the theoretical discussion of Chapter 1, arguing that the linguist's reconstruction of our role as readers may give clues about the nature of literature. After all, the linguist himself is only a rather specialized kind of reader.

A characterization of linguistics that I have sometimes toyed with is 'a non-prescriptive Rhetoric'. Puttenham did his linguistic stylistics very well, it might be thought, and much of our present job is the development of a metalanguage—a way of talking about language—as comprehensive as his. G. N. Leech's 'Linguistics and the Figures of Rhetoric' is an essay in the interpretation of the old system in terms of the new: not an exercise in terminological translation, but an attempt 'to suggest how linguistic *theory* can be accommodated to the task of describing such recurrent phenomena in literature as metaphor, parallelism, alliteration and antithesis'.

Two studies by medievalists conclude the volume. We have given space to two medieval topics (by colleagues whose ideas have assisted me greatly in deciding the shape of the book) in acknowledgment of the already fruitful association of critical and linguistic studies in the description and interpretation of medieval literature. J. Norton-Smith, with a problem of literary history, demonstrates the value of close textual analysis and comparison in settling questions of genre and source. R. F. Lawrence, following an increasingly fertile line of investigation into the characteristics of oral poetry, describes and comments upon some approaches to the formulae of English alliterative poetry.

These observations on 'something in common' and 'novel' lead me to an attempt to summarize the purpose of this book as it has now developed. The original contributors are glad to find that there is no single thing 'linguistic stylistics' that they can describe. We hope that the book will indicate some of the range of approaches to literary language that are current today; some of the ways linguists and critics can communicate, use each other's ideas, in a subject until recently on the fringes of both linguistic and literary studies; some of the stylistic uses to which linguistic data can be put. If our book encourages more experiment and discussion and some studies in greater depth than we can allow here, we may believe that we have helped to lessen parochialism as well as enliven our own parishes.

Many friends and colleagues have interested themselves in the collection or in particular essays. I am especially indebted to the advice of past colleagues in the University of Hull, who encouraged and corrected freely: especially to Professor R. L. Brett, David Palmer and T. E. McAlindon; to Professor Donald Charlton, now of the University of Warwick.

My fellow-contributors have read each other's chapters in a long series of drafts, and I know that they have also submitted their ideas to other specialists in Edinburgh, London, Manchester and Nottingham.

ROGER FOWLER

1

Linguistic Theory and the Study of Literature

IN THIS CENTURY, students of language and literature have witnessed the development of a new discipline, linguistics, to a state of relative maturity. The development has been marked by a progressive growth in the number of books and persons attached to the subject, and so it is ceasing to be something rather esoteric, and is finding a place among the established humanities. Unfortunately, one feels that the integration of linguistics with its natural companion, literary criticism, has been hindered by something unsympathetic in the way the linguist has presented himself. The image is sometimes an unhappy one: pretension of scientific accuracy; obsession with an extensive, cumbersome and recondite terminology; display of analytic techniques; scorn of all that is subjective, impressionistic, mentalistic—in a word, 'prelinguistic'. But this view of the linguist—armed to the teeth and potentially destructive by his attack on a sensitive work of art—cannot be substantiated: it rarely has any factual basis in the actual practices and interests of linguists.

Just as there is no single thing 'literary criticism' which produces a 'critic' who can be identified by reference to his methods and beliefs, so linguistics as a homogeneous, evangelical, operative-producing subject does not exist. We cannot altogether predict a linguist's attitude to his analysis of a text. There is no one linguistic method with easily characterizable modes of operation and endproducts. Certain fundamentals are common to all who call themselves linguists: the beliefs that language changes, is patterned, is only conventionally connected with the outside world, and has an analysable form, for example. But when we look closer we find fewer agreements on details. The history of linguistics reveals tentative effort, revisions of opinion, lack of universal continuous progress. There have been, as in the development of any new discipline, independent schools of linguists: following Bloomfield, Chomsky, Hjelmslev, for example. There is diversification within the field of language studies independent of adherence to general theories: a linguist to the world may be, to his colleagues, a phonetician, dialectologist, grammarian, lexicographer. There is disagreement on the relationship between linguistics and other subjects: is it a social science, a physical science, a humanity? is it most closely related to literary criticism, sociology, psychology, philosophy? We cannot, it seems, be sure what is meant by 'linguistics' in a title like that of the present chapter, nor what the author intends to produce when he places linguistics *vis-à-vis* literature. A linguistic analysis of a literary text could, judging by some precedents, be exclusively grammatical, or metrical, or lexical, or phonetic, and, whichever of these emphases governs it, it could use the language of any one of a number of existing forms of linguistics. In effect, most linguistic analyses of a text of whatever kind will be linguistic by virtue of certain fundamental tenets common to all linguists since de Saussure. Variation of detail in the techniques and terminology will depend on selection of a particular school of linguistics to be followed.

Today, perhaps more than at any other time in the twentieth century, there may be great uncertainty in our decision as to what linguistics is. We are conscious of great differences between our ways of thinking and those of our predecessors in the formative years of 'classic' linguistics before the Second World War. We are, it is hoped, less likely to champion one school exclusively. Almost everyone must be familiar with the basic texts of the major schools of thought: not only Bloomfield, Sapir and de Saussure, but Harris, Chomsky, Firth, Hjemslev and Jakobson. Linguists of different persuasions are in close contact through reciprocal visits between England and America. The post-war years have seen developments outside as well as within our field which could not have failed to influence. Acoustic phonetics has increased enormously the precision with which the sounds of utterances can be described, and has necessitated a new look at the way we interpret vocal noises as meaningful activity. Communication theory, methods of quantifying information, and statistical procedures have provided new ways of analysing and talking about language. Machine translation has made demands on our ingenuity in the compilation of grammars and vocabularies for this specialized use. The war itself, bringing a sudden need for intensive language-teaching activity, provided an impetus to pure and applied linguistics. Yet more changes in the field of linguistics are moving us in new directions. In this country, the expansion of linguistics as a university subject, and improved facilities for communication between linguists (principally the formation of the Linguistics Association) have led to the corporate building up of a new linguistics much indebted to the late Professor Firth. In America, a mode of analysis which is certainly new and which has been hailed as revolutionary (transformation-generative grammar) has grown up in less than ten years.

So, in 1965, linguistics is a huge, diverse cluster of subjects of complex historical origin and evidently in a period of great change: the conception of it as a set, arid, insensitive and limited group of stereotyped techniques is a fiction. In my title is implied no question of an established and unprogressive linguistics moving in on a field outside its competence; rather, it is a developing discipline hoping to learn about language by turning its attention to those texts called 'literary', and in the process exploring its relation with literary criticism, with which it has in common a basic concern with the uses of language.

The current desire to investigate literary uses of language should be seen in a historical setting: as the end of a series of alternations in the interest of language students in texts of different character. One of the early influences on the rise of twentieth-century linguistics was reaction against the past, specifically against lack of interest in spoken language and against preoccupation with highly valued examples of written language. So (to oversimplify somewhat) we find nineteenth-century philologists interested predominantly in written texts, despite the great advances in linguistic methods made in that century, and on the other hand the writers of prescriptive grammars persisting in basing their comments on the language on the forms of written documents, advocating the imitation of 'classic' literary works. Against this (and additionally because of their concern with the unwritten languages of the indigenous peoples of America) American linguists erected the principle that speech is the primary form of language. Written language, it was argued, is a derived system, based on speech and coming after speech in the development of both civilizations and individuals. We find countless examples of definitions of language framed deliberately to exclude written language, of grammars which claim to be based entirely on spoken forms. This attitude leads to an implied denigration of written language, to a view of peculiarly literary forms as modifications of 'normal usage'. One type of normative grammar was replaced by its converse. It is not until the 'fifties that we find evidence of a swing away from this position. American linguists/anthropologists had long interested themselves in the oral literatures of non-literate peoples—often in the correlation between cultural factors and the selection of deviant, characteristically literary, features. Circumstances in the 'fifties were particularly favourable to making the step from oral literature to written texts, involving as it did giving less prominence to the 'primacy of speech' principle and recognizing that, in fact, much past analysis of so-called colloquial texts had treated material which often manifested grammatical forms not particularly associated with spoken language. In the last few years, some discussions of literary texts by linguists attracted attention to the applicability of linguistic techniques to literature, and there have also been a number of general or theoretical essays.[1] At the same time some literary critics came to acknowledge the

[1] For example, A. A. Hill, 'An Analysis of *The Windhover:* An Experiment in Structural Method', *PMLA*, lxx (1955), 968–78; Seymour Chatman, 'Robert Frost's "Mowing": An Inquiry into Prosodic Structure', *Kenyon Review*, xviii (1956), 421–38; T. A. Sebeok (ed.), *Style in Language* (MIT, 1960), *passim;* S. R. Levin, *Linguistic Structures in Poetry, Janua Linguarum*, xxiii (The Hague, 1962); N. Ruwet, 'L'analyse structurale de la poésie', *Linguistics*, ii (December 1963), 33–59.

necessity for the close study of the language of literature.[2] In these recent years, also, developments in linguistic theory have directed attention to problems of great interest in literary studies. For example, in *Language* for 1952 Z. S. Harris gave an outline of a new form of linguistic description, 'discourse analysis', one of the cardinal points of which is its interest in those distributions of linguistic elements which link sentences within a text. Previously, linguists had taken the sentence, a relatively small unit, as their upper limit of magnitude for description; now, methods of analysis were promised which dealt with stretches of language longer than the sentence. Now perhaps linguistics could move to a consideration of formal devices, including patterns in literature, which tended to unify or structure continuous texts. Again, we find in the writings of Chomsky in the late 'fifties a concern with the question of grammaticalness—with the status of utterances like *colorless green ideas sleep furiously* in relation to the grammar of English. As such utterances are more likely within literature than outside it, Chomsky was in fact approaching some facets of literary expression. It appears (e.g. from the discussion in Sebeok's *Style in Language*) that the Chomskyan notion of 'degrees of grammaticalness' is of no slight importance in the study of literary language. Finally we should mention the very recent development, chiefly by British linguists, of ways of discussing *lexis* (vocabulary), especially the study of combinations of lexical items (*collocations*); a development which takes some of the load off grammar in the description of forms of expression. All three linguistic interests are symptomatic of the linguist's growing desire to increase his range.

I mentioned above changes in the attitudes of linguists to the relation of written to spoken language. One view was that literature is characterized by formal features different from the conventions of spoken or colloquial usage. This argument was used in the past to justify concentration on spoken language ('normal' or 'common' usage) alone. But it is also one which

[2] For example, Donald Davie, *Articulate Energy* (London, 1955); Christine Brooke-Rose, *A Grammar of Metaphor* (London, 1958); Winifred Nowottny, *The Language Poets Use* (London, 1962).

deserves consideration on its own account, as one of the several possible views of the relation between literary and non-literary forms of discourse. We should now look at some of these views, implying as they do the definition of literature.

Several relationships, and sets of terms, are involved in this basic question: written language and spoken language, literature and non-literature, common usage and literature, poetry and literature. The simplest opposition is between written and spoken realizations of language, and the chief difference is the obvious one: that speech and writing employ different media for the transmission of messages. One works through noises in the air, the other through marks on paper or other material. These means of transmission are termed *substance* by linguists.[3] Substance is only the surface of language, and I introduce it only as a linguistic category with which we are not really concerned. It is the province of phonetics, or calligraphy, or typography. The linguist and literary critic need to go deeper than this. There are in fact other characteristic differences between speech and writing. They are not translatable into each other simply by changing their substance. This chapter cannot be turned into speech merely by reading it aloud: if this is done, it will be found to exhibit formal characteristics (i.e. linguistic features at a deeper level than substance) which would not be found in a sample of speech which had not been 'translated' from written language. Conversely, a written translation of an informal conversation will not fulfil one's expectations of the forms of prose. That there are formal as well as substantial differences is attributable partly to the circumstances attendant upon the selection of either phonic or graphic substance: the greater speed and spontaneity of speech; the consideration of permanence of the written word; in the case of writing, the prescriptive training and the consultation of normative models in our education and reading—only rarely is specific training given in speech. But more influential in making speech and writing differ formally is what Mr Leech (Chapter 8)

[3] Most of the technical terms I use are current usage among linguists in Great Britain, and are to be found in M. A. K. Halliday, 'Categories of the Theory of Grammar', *Word*, xvii (1961), 241–92.

calls the *register scale*. Differences of form between speech and writing may, it is true, often be accounted for by factors just linked to the difference in substance; but more powerful in determining formal features—irrespective of realization in substance—is the place an utterance occupies on the register scale. Spoken utterances differ formally from written because they are, typically, used in different communication situations and for different purposes: for calling a dog, comforting a child, ordering a meal, but rarely for annotating a text, giving a recipe, making a will. I shall return later to the register scale, the scale of situations and functions which governs the selection of forms, and treat it as a selective principle overriding the distinction between speech and writing; but this distinction does occur at a definite point in the scale: some groups of situations select written substance and characteristic forms, while others tend to select phonic substance and another set of forms.

Poems have the characteristic that while they are most usually originally realized in written form, their reading is often a spoken one. We need not consider the question of whether a poem is designed as a spoken utterance and committed to writing only as a guarantee of permanence (but some poems, for example some by George Herbert or by Dylan Thomas, have visual form independent of their phonology). Professor Firth considered that all written texts have 'implication of utterance', and this is certainly a necessary assumption in the study of metrics. We need note only that poetic texts rather than any others may exist in both types of substantial realization—phonic and graphic. The problem is to determine what aspects of phonic substance are part of the poem, and what are to be relegated to the reading only. As several readings of the poem may offer many phonetic variations, the question is a vital one: in many phonetically (substantially) different readings, in what sense is the poem repeated? what features of the readings are part of the poem, and what are merely the embellishments of the recitation? Four roughly corresponding pairs of terms are available to aid our thinking over this. General linguistic theory provides *langue* vs. *parole* (de Saussure's distinction between the language as an abstract system and speech as an individual act of articulation), and *form* vs. *substance* (current British usage making a similar distinction, form being an abstraction made from substance). C. S. Peirce's distinction of *type* from *token* has sometimes been adopted to distinguish between a linguistic unit (e.g. 'poem') and its realizations. Finally, some of the contributors to Sebeok's *Style in Language* spoke of *message* vs. *performance*. *Message* is an unfortunate term, carrying its more usual connotations of 'information carried by an utterance'. *Performance* is a useful word in connexion with recitation. All these pairs of terms serve to distinguish a poem 'which constitutes a replicable, invariant structure' from 'its acoustic implementation in the concrete performance' (Edward Stankiewicz, Sebeok, p. 75). Stankiewicz goes on:

> Every poem constitutes a specific type, composed of invariable elements, whereas the various deliveries constitute its tokens. A poem is, in other words, an organized message, the elements of which must recur in any performance. The study of these constant elements alone constitutes the science of versification, whereas the study of the variations of delivery (where we may, in turn, discern certain dominant types) constitutes the art of declamation. To the modern linguist the distinction between these two branches appears similar to that between phonemics and phonetics.

(Cf. Hollander, Sebeok, p. 191; Wimsatt and Beardsley, Sebeok, p. 193; Wellek and Warren, *Theory of Literature* [3rd ed., Harmondsworth 1963], p. 158.)

I shall summarize my view of this distinction, using three of the available terms. A poem (like any utterance) has *form*, which is invariant and repeatable; form is the proper object of study for stylistics, as for linguistics; it has describable meaning on various sublevels. It can be realized in two ways, both of which are *substance*: as a written record (e.g. the poet's written record, or the transcription of a poem of oral origin) or as a spoken recitation. As poetry, of all literary utterances, demands recitation, it is useful to signify this by the use of a special term, *performance*. A performance, although most usually stimulated by a reading of written substance, is not to be viewed as an implementation of the written record (although the metaphor of 'translation of substance' might be useful in some circumstances) but an independent realization; because the written record is not the poem, but is itself only an implementation of it. The distinction is not between the poem on paper and the reading of it but between the poem (an abstraction) and two ways of realizing it.

Some linguistic features are readily ascribable to form, some to performance. Dialect variation is a feature of performance—as Seymour Chatman says, Hamlet speaking with a North Georgia accent is still Hamlet. So are the 'vocal qualifiers': expressive features such as overloudness, oversoftness, drawling, variations of tempo. It has been argued that prosodic features (stress, intonation) are features of performance, because they are imperfectly signalled in a written text and therefore variable in a performance. Under form we place grammar, vocabulary, the segmental phonemes (those distinctive sounds of a language that are placed in linear sequence), and perhaps such prosodic features as are unambiguously indicated by the grammar or the evident metrical convention. Metrics is the area of most doubtful allocation, and indeed the distinction between message or form and performance has been made (as by Stankiewicz) specifically to clarify the position of metre (optional or invariable?). The point remains doubtful; but the distinction is certainly worth making as it directs attention to aspects of poetic form which are unquestionably open to linguistic investigation.

The existence of oral literature (e.g. folk-narratives) and of written non-literature (e.g. telephone directories) makes it obvious that the distinction between the two domains is not that between speech and writing. Even if it did happen that some society had no oral literature and no written non-literature we would consider this distinction either fortuitous or useless. Neither the linguist nor the literary critic is interested in mere difference of substance: language is *form*, not the physical representation of form.

Substance gives no clue to the difference between literature and non-literature. At first glance it might seem that formal characteristics might serve to identify literature—rhyme, metre, alliteration, unusual collocations, repetitions of grammatical structure. But within literature these are most frequent in poetry, so will not be infallible in identifying all literature. Moreover, they will be found outside literature (e.g. repetition of grammatical pattern in inventories, telephone directories, etc.) so they will not identify literature only. One characterization of literature (or at least of poetry) which has rested on formal features concerns not individual points but wider aspects of organization. So colloquial English may be said to be formless, haphazard, disjointed, incomplete, whereas literature is highly organized and finished. Winifred Nowottny (*The Language Poets Use*, p. 72) suggests that 'the chief difference between language in poems and language outside poems is that the one is more highly structured than the other'. For others 'normal' or 'common' usage is the regular basis of a language, and its literature has the privilege of breaking the rules—poetic licence—and thrives by the exploitation of formal individuality to produce startling collocations or departures from ordinary grammar. Unexciting but more realistic is the view that different types of utterance are marked by different rules of structure within the permitted ranges of the whole language, and that there are not just two categories, one deviant from the other.

It is unlikely that any formal feature, or set of features, can be found, the presence or absence of which will unequivocally identify literature. Put another way, there is probably no absolute formal distinction between literature and non-literature: neither of these two categories is formally homogeneous. This conclusion must be of prime importance to the linguist, for it relieves him of the necessity of making special assumptions about the nature of literary form. The form of utterances designated 'literary' is assumed to hold no special problems consequent upon the designation as literature—it is just linguistic form. This must not be misunderstood, interpreted as a denial of the existence of literature. It is a working hypothesis necessary for the linguist, an assumption that all examples of language have a linguistic form susceptible of investigation. The designation 'literature' for one class of utterances makes no difference to this situation, for it seems that, while members of this class exhibit both formal differences among themselves and differences from the forms of types of utterances outside the class, there is no constant, or set of constants, which differentiates all members of the class 'literature' from all members of the class 'non-literature'.

It is probably a fruitless task to attempt to define literature by any criteria, formal or otherwise—just as our recognition of what texts are literary is unreliable in borderline cases (e.g. in the decision whether to call a text 'bad literature' or 'non-literature' but not in discriminating between Yeats and the instructions on a cake-mix packet); and an absolute, self-evident distinction is belied by changes in tastes and individual differences of opinion. Northrop Frye asserts (*Anatomy of Criticism*, p. 13): 'We have no real standards to distinguish a verbal structure that is literary from one that is not, and no idea what to do with the vast penumbra of books that may be claimed for literature because they are written with "style", or are useful as "background", or have simply got into a university course of "great books".' The most illuminating criteria are probably contextual, not formal.[4] Contextual features may be invoked to explain why we use the label 'literature' at a certain time for a certain text; to rationalize our recognition of a text as literature, rather than to define absolutely what the general phenomenon of literature is. I do not intend to go into this at any length, because I have stated the restriction of my field of study to linguistic form. But some suggestions may be noted. C. F. Voegelin (Sebeok, pp. 57–68) makes a distinction between *casual* and *non-casual* texts, not exactly equalling that between non-literature and literature, but designed to throw light on this dichotomy. Non-casual utterances, he suggests, are restricted by the society in which they occur to certain times and places—their contexts are carefully controlled; casual utterances have freer distribution. Further, 'neither formal training nor specialized interest contributes . . . to the proficiency of different varieties of casual utterances'. (See Roman Jakobson, Sebeok, p. 351, for an objection to Voegelin's distinction.) A. A. Hill suggests and then discards permanence as a criterion for

[4] There is some variation of usage in the general terms used for extra-linguistic aspects of language: *context*, or *situation*, or *context of situation* in British linguistics; *macro-linguistic*, *exolinguistic* and others in American usage.

literature; related to this is the motive for desiring permanence, the belief in the non-utilitarian value of literary texts. Rephrasing this, we say that literary texts are, characteristically, realized frequently by oral or other reading, whereas non-literary utterances tend to be unique or at least transitory. The necessity of repetition is given great weight by Martin Joos ('The Five Clocks', *IJAL*, xxviii [1962], 33): 'Literature is that text which the community insists on having repeated from time to time intact.' Another norm which has been invoked is that of fictionality, elaborated by René Wellek, who implies the irrelevance to literature of the criterion of true vs. false: 'Take the telephone book. This is distinct from literature not because it's true but because it is not worthwhile using except in respect to it's [*sic*] being true or not true' (Sebeok, p. 101). Wellek and Warren (*Theory of Literature*, pp. 25–6) discuss further the notion of fictionality, and make a point of interest to stylistics: 'If we recognize "fictionality", "invention", or "imagination" as the distinguishing trait of literature, we think thus of literature in terms of Homer, Dante, Shakespeare, Balzac, Keats rather than of Cicero, Montaigne, Bossuet, or Emerson.' That is to say, such a view of literature is less kind to the 'stylists' than to 'imaginative' writers and even writers of narrative. And it perhaps minimizes the place of stylistics in literary criticism. Contrast the view of some linguists that the form of poetry 'acquires autonomous value' (Stankiewicz, Sebeok, p. 75): it draws attention to itself, becomes an end in itself, by either (depending on one's angle) being more highly organized or more deviant than ordinary language. However, these opinions on the importance of form in literature make no difference to the fact that linguistic form exists and is the primary area of investigation in all examples of language.

From the above, it would seem that the linguist should be concerned only with the form of texts, and that he should not consider the status of a text as literature as a necessary datum prior to his analysis. The allocation of a text to the class 'literature' is a matter of context; even though the linguist may find that the presence of one set of formal features tends to correlate with the label 'literature', he will also find sets that characterize either literature or non-literature. And yet the linguist will want to hypothesize the selection of different forms according to varying contextual circumstances. He will want to recognize the principle of difference of style determined by difference of situation and function which is implied in such phrases as 'the language of sermons', 'the language of advertising'. This is a question of taking account of the influence of *register* on *style*, of which I shall say more shortly.

In order to accommodate such a flexible and potentially minute means of classification as a scale, we have to do away with the absolute distinction between literature and everything else. I have suggested that the label 'literature' yields a class which is so heterogeneous as to make the name minimally useful: all critics are very quickly forced to subdivide—plays, poems, novels, lyrics, etc. If 'literature' is a vague term, 'non-literature' hardly helps us to define literature by contrast, as it itself is a term of too wide applicability. We have to oppose to literature not only ordinary speech—an opposition found in classic discussions of poetic diction—but the language of weather forecasts, learned articles, crossword-puzzle clues, news bulletins. If these are not literature, then they are certainly not 'common usage', which turns out to be a mirage. Nor are they 'borderline cases'. These also stand unresolved by the dichotomy: we are in no doubt about Shakespeare's sonnets or *How to fill in your income tax form*, but the opposition hardly helps us to agree on articles in *Punch* or the *New Yorker*. We could not profit by simply substituting a scale for the dichotomy, even though it would honestly face the fact that there are genuine borderline utterances. No sort of *contextual* scale could easily be free from criteria of value. For example, I think immediately of a scale with literature as the top. What is at the bottom? Bad literature or non-literature? I hesitate to suggest examples as I cannot see how such a scale can help us to determine the order of occurrence of non-literary utterances.

Saporta (Sebeok, p. 99), objecting to the simple literature/non-literature distinction as I am doing, suggests: 'Instead of looking for such a dichotomy, it may be feasible to order messages along a continuum; or at least if the categories are to be discrete, it may be possible to provide more than two of them.' I have argued that a continuum of contextual identification is not possible, but wish to proceed later to explore the idea of formal continua. As for discrete categories, more than two in number, this is a solution which has application on both of the levels, form and context. Enough examples may easily be collected to suggest that there is certainly a large number of context-defined classes, and that form-defined classes may tend to coincide with them. In brief, contextual variety within a society results in formal variety within its language, and the variety is of a sort which cannot be adequately recognized by a two-class categorization of texts. As Professor Quirk puts it (*The Use of English* [London, 1962], p. 19): 'every particular *use* of English is to some extent reflected in and determines the *form* of the language that is used for that particular purpose'.

We must now take cognizance of the relation between form and context by introducing the notions of the language as a whole, style, and register. The first, on the level of context, embraces all functions of a particular language, or, more broadly, all utterances considered as complex wholes functioning on all levels. On the level of substance, it embraces both main media and perhaps other derived media, such as semaphore and phonetic script. On the level of form, it embraces all possible types of formal organization. All native speakers of an individual language must be assumed to have a relatively high proficiency in varieties within the language. Nearly everyone can speak and understand speech; many can write and read. Most people are either actively or passively proficient in a large number of varieties of their language. Speakers of different dialects can converse by virtue of their common possession of formal rules fundamental to most dialects of the language, and by virtue of their ability to understand these basic rules variously interpreted by different speakers. Everyone commands many different forms for use in different situations, and understands a great many more that he himself does not use actively.

A set of contextual features bringing about a characteristic use of formal features may be called a *register*. (This term has been defined more precisely, e.g. by Professor Barbara Strang, *Modern English Structure* [London, 1962], pp. 19–20, with reference to variety of social roles only.) The sum of the resultant formal characteristics may be called a *style*. The interplay of the two notions is implied in such phrases as 'the language of . . . ' where *language* means 'style' and the blank is filled by a reference to the register in question. A few examples may be given. The language of telephone conversations is marked by a large number of occurrences of the formal item *yes*; the same feature is found in conversations where someone is giving instructions to someone else. The language of advertising, for obvious contextual reasons peculiar to the register, requires the constant use of the lexical item *new* in certain positions and of certain other lexical items (e.g. words with favourable connotations) and grammatical forms (e.g. comparative and superlative adjectives). The language of poetry is most often characterized by repetition of phonological features at certain points of time: isochronous stress, alliteration, rhyme. The languages of specialized disciplines are marked by the use of special vocabulary items not of widespread distribution in the language as a whole. The style of court circulars and social announcement columns in newspapers has a high density of one class of lexical items, proper names. The register employed by a parent talking to its child often has a small vocabulary, a small range of grammatical constructions (with imperatives prominent) and perhaps idiosyncratic phonological conventions.

Style—a property of *all* texts, not just literary—may be said to reside in the manipulation of variables in the structure of a language, or in the selection of optional or 'latent' features. As a theoretical prerequisite to stylistic study we assume that there are both constant and variable features within 'the language as a whole'. The constants are the rules of the language which make styles and dialects *within one language* possible. One constant, for English, is the complex set of rules determining the orders and positions in which phonemes can occur. /ʒ/ and /ŋ/ (as in mea*s*ure and si*ng*) cannot occur at the beginnings of words, except in quotations from foreign languages—*j*oie, *N*krumah. There are elaborate rules governing the combinations of consonants permitted in different positions: for example, /tl-/, /rk-/ cannot occur initially, but /kl-/, /skr-/ can. However, there are no rules governing the frequency with which individual phonemes may occur in a text, or requiring them to occur periodically. The phoneme /f/ can be distributed rarely and haphazardly, as in *French is the second language of some Englishmen*, or frequently and deliberately, as in *the furrow followed free*.[5] Rules of word-order required Donne (in *The Will*) to write *Before I sigh my last gaspe*, not *gaspe last I before sigh my; let me breath . . . some Legacies*, not *some me breath Legacies let*. But he was free to put the clauses together in either order, and to fit in *Great love* almost anywhere he wished. Stylistic considerations (e.g. his favoured trick of starting a poem with a subordinate clause) alone contrived to make him manipulate clause-order rules to produce:

> Before I sigh my last gaspe, let me breath,
> Great love, some Legacies . . .

Lexis is perhaps the level of linguistic form at which variables can be treated with the greatest freedom and are of most significance for stylistic study. This level differs from grammar and phonology in comprising an inventory of items which is indefinitely extensible. Perhaps more important for stylistics is the fact that, while grammar and phonology consist of finite sets of items which are the possession of all users of a language, the vocabulary of the whole language is more extensive than that of any one speaker or any one register. A register may often be characterized by reference to its vocabulary alone—for example the specialized jargons of the so-called occupational dialects. In some positions in an utterance there is a virtually infinite range of possibilities of lexical occurrence. In the sentence *The book was on the table*, the rules of grammar dictate that the grammatical unit noun must occur between *The* and *was*; but the choice of a lexical exponent of the noun is vast: *book*, *pen*, *notepaper*, *tablecloth*, etc. A. A. Hill, with this lexical freedom in mind, comments:

[5] So the study of the frequencies of phonemes is a part of stylistics. See James J. Lynch, 'The Tonality of Lyric Poetry', *Word*, ix (1953); Dell H. Hymes, 'Phonological Aspects of Style: Some English Sonnets', Sebeok, pp. 109–31; Francis Berry, *Poetry and the Physical Voice* (London, 1962), pp. 98–9.

'some students prefer to describe stylistics as the sum total of choices, which the language offers to the individual speaker, at each point within the sentence.'[6] Of course, stylistics involves phonology and grammar as well as lexis; if we remember this and the principle of variables, we may agree that Hill's remark sums up much of our interest in stylistics.

But we must go beyond the sentence. It is a commonplace among linguists that the sentence is the upper limit of magnitude in linguistic analysis, and the fact that stylistics must deal with larger units has been taken as a major difference between linguistics and stylistics: 'whereas the maximum unit in linguistics is the sentence, a larger unit, the text, serves as the basis of stylistic analysis' (Saporta, Sebeok, p. 88).[7] We are not interested in this question as a criterion in setting up an opposition between linguistics and stylistics; the position taken here is that stylistics is a branch of linguistics, but one concerned especially with the treatment of variables in entire texts. Linguistic relations between sentences in a continuous text may be studied (in an informal way at least) regardless of the presumed non-existence of linguistic units larger than the sentence. If linguistic relations above the sentence are assumed to be 'free', this is to say that they are in fact linguistic variables and therefore the concern of stylistics. Winifred Nowottny comments (*The Language Poets Use*, p. 73): 'The structure even of ordinary language is, above the level of the sentence, "free", so far as linguistic analysis is concerned.' She quotes J. L. M. Trim: 'Above the sentence, permitted sequence is so free that no attempt is made to state the possibilities. Any substantial sequence of sentences will probably constitute a unique utterance.' If grammar above the sentence is a free-choice area it will thus, like lexis, be of great interest in stylistics. Linguistic investigation of orders of types of sentences, repetitive devices covering extensive pieces of text, and so on, could be of considerable importance to literary criticism, dealing with a field of study

[6] 'A Program for the Definition of Literature', *University of Texas Studies in English* xxxvii (1958), 50.

[7] Cf. S. R. Levin, *Linguistic Structures in Poetry*, pp. 11–12 and references. On the sentence as the 'largest' unit in English, see Fowler, 'Sentence and Clause in English,' *Linguistics*, xiv (1965), 5–13.

that criticism, like linguistics, has hitherto neglected. Much research needs to be done into unifying devices in continuous texts, the nature of verse paragraphs, the internal linguistic structure of novels.

For an example of greater-than-sentence stylistics, we take Bacon's essay *Of Studies* (1625 version). Several devices work for the unification of this text. An obvious one is the lexical trick of repeating one word many times. The noun *study/studies* occurs six times; the verb *study* three. This may be taken as a trivial point (and it is); but there was no linguistic constraint on the writer to use one lexical item nine times: he has added to the homogeneity of his paragraph by doing so. One of the provisions the language does make for connecting sentences is the availability of pronouns to link with antecedents in preceding sentences or clauses. Bacon is seen to exploit this very fully: the pronoun *they/them/their*, referring to *studies*, is used eleven times. Another unifying device is consistency of tense. Bacon uses the present throughout this essay, and almost exclusively in his others—it may be thought that there is a particular connection between the present tense and the essay genre in this period. By far the most impressive of the unifying features is Bacon's use of a tripartite scheme in his grammatical constructions. Three-unit structures are not fundamental to English, except in one statistically frequent type of clause, the subject-predicator-complement type (e.g. *John loves Mary*). The rules of English do not force Bacon to have three items in his opening *for Delight, for Ornament, and for Ability*. In starting this pattern he launches on an effective but rare rhetorical scheme; compare the much greater popularity of schemes based on two- or four-fold grammatical repetition (Lyly and most other balanced or antithetical prose). As the essay progresses, he gives the following patterns:

1. Three phrases: for Delight
for Ornament
and for Ability.

2. One clause, plus two partial expansions of a clause:
Their Chiefe Use for Delight, is in Priuatenesse and Retiring

For Ornament, is in Discourse
And for Ability, in the Iudgement and Disposition of Businesse.

3. Three nominal groups:

the generall Counsells
and the Plots
and Marshalling of Affaires.

4. Three clauses:

To spend too much Time in *Studies*, is Sloth
To vse them too much for Ornament, is Affectation
To make Iudgement wholly by their Rules is the Humour of a Scholler.

5. Three clauses:

Crafty Men Contemne *Studies*
Simple Men Admire them
and Wise Men Vse them.

6. as 2:

Some bookes are to be Tasted
Others to be Swallowed
and Some Few to be Chewed and Digested.

7. as 2 and 6:

Some *Bookes* are to be read onely in Parts
Others to be read but not Curiously
and some Few to be read wholly, and with Diligence and Attention.

8. as 2, 6 and 7:

Reading maketh a Full Man
Conference a Ready Man
and Writing an Exact Man.

9. Three 'complex sentences':

If a Man write little, he had need haue a Great memory
If he Conferre little, he had need haue a Present Wit
and if he Reade litle, he had need haue much Cunning . . .

10. as 9:

> So if a Mans Wit be Wandering, let him *Study* the *Mathematicks* . . .
> If his Wit be not Apt to distinguish or find differences, let him *Study* the *Schoolemen* . . .
> If he be not Apt to beat Ouer Matters . . . let him *Study* the *Lawyers Cases* . . .

Bacon clearly builds his paragraph around three-part structures. The structures are not required by the grammar; in fact, it is difficult to describe in linguistic terms what he has done, for there are no linguistic terms available for units and patterns larger than the sentence. 'Repetition' is involved, but it is not repetition of any one unit, but of a pattern present in a number of different units. I have been at pains to demonstrate that, in terms of grammar, there is not just repetition of one unit—in fact, five different grammatical forms carry the pattern. It is this *pattern* that is repeated, and it must be called a 'stylistic' or 'rhetorical' pattern: a pattern most usually only latent, or accidentally present, in utterances, but here forced into our view by Bacon's manipulation of variables which are not required by the grammar and which work together to produce textual coherence.

It must be emphasized that the primary unit for stylistic description is a whole text seen as a unit, not as a string of sentences. At the present stage of the development of descriptive linguistics, with its marked orientation towards the sentence as the unit for description, there will inevitably be concentration, at the level of grammar, on small units within the text. Analysis of sentence-structure and of the structure of lower-rank units is both a procedural necessity and a necessary foundation for stylistics: but grammatical structures should then be seen in relation to the whole text and to the other constituents of the text, not only in relation to comparable structures in other texts or in 'the language as a whole'. The linguist C. F. Hockett has argued that a poem is a long idiom: an utterance with a total meaning which is not merely the sum of the meanings of its separate components. So an account of a poem cannot be merely an inventory of its parts, however minutely analysed, but must involve also a statement of the network of relations between the parts, even though (as in the Bacon passage) the relation might not appear to be susceptible of conventional linguistic description. A literary critic's paraphrase is given by Mrs Nowottny (op. cit., p. 18): 'meaning and value in poems are the product of a whole array of elements of language, all having a potential of eloquence which comes to realization when, and only when, one element is set in discernible relation with another . . . '. The linguist must make a *whole* analysis of the literary text, and must then proceed to utilize his analysed and understood fragments as elements in a synthesis. Relations within each level must be explored. For example, the linguist must relate his isolated grammatical statements to one another: in my treatment of *Of Studies*, I was concerned to relate thrice-repeated phrases, not with thrice-repeated phrases outside the essay, but with three-fold repetition of all types of grammatical unit within the essay. Again, the linguist engaged in stylistics must be prepared to describe points of contact between the levels of form: to connect lexical with grammatical, grammatical with phonological, details. In Chapter 5 we will discuss one inter-level relationship, that between grammar and phonology, as it bears on one area of stylistics, metrics.

The comparison of the stylistic features of two or more texts is a distinct and logically secondary activity. We may be interested in a text only for the sake of that text itself, as I have described above; but the results of this analysis may be compared with those of an analysis (which must be carried out on similar principles) of another text. In the first activity, the repetition 3× (preposition +noun) (*for Delight, for Ornament, and for Ability*) is viewed as significant in relation to all the other 3× repetitions in this one passage. In the second, the structure may be connected with other examples: for example, it appears once in *Of Studies*, and might appear more frequently, or not at all, in a text of similar length which is being compared. Now this is a very different type of observation from the one I made originally, and I might have one of two motives for making it. It could be argued that the frequency of occurrence of any linguistic from in a text is significant only by comparison with its frequency in other texts: it is degree of deviation which gives it value. The total for a single text could be considered meaningless, and would continue meaningless if it were found to be the same as the total for all other texts. The assumption behind such an argument is that usage in one text is significant only by comparison with usage outside it: our reaction to Thomas's phrase *once below a time*, or *farmyards away*, is conditioned by our past experience of *once upon a time* and *miles away*; alliteration (periodicity of repeated phonemes) strikes us because most of the time we do not encounter alliteration. Of course this is true—we respond to a poem in the light of our past experience of the styles of many other registers, at the same time as we respond to it on the basis of its own linguistic components. I do not wish to challenge this notion of deviation if it is intended to present (probably statistically) information which models our own automatic procedure of comparison. But it should not replace completely the other approach, the description of a text as a complete and unique unit; nor should it always invite comparison between a particular literary usage and usage in the elusive 'normal speech'. Total dependence on the idea of deviation may lead us to the unsatisfactory general view of poetry as language deviant from normal usage, not (the view I take) as part of the language as a whole. We should not see all poetry as a poetic licence, language modified and twisted.

A second motive for comparing the treatment of the same structure in two texts might be stylistic comparison, for its own sake or for any of several purposes in the study of literary history (arguments about authorship, stylistic 'schools', genres). Here we do not assume a difference between the style of text A and normal style; we assume that there is a multitude of styles corresponding to a multitude of registers, and that any two or more of these may be compared with respect to any linguistic feature or features. We should recall our replacement of the dichotomy literature: non-literature or literature: normal usage by a continuum of texts of all sorts, or if not a continuum a very large number of separate types of texts. Corresponding to the register scale is one on which texts are identified by stylistic rather than contextual features. Now, it is difficult to imagine how to order texts, seen as complexes of many stylistic features, on a continuum or even a simple scale. The style of a text (from the point of view of comparison, as well as of the text seen as an autonomous unit) is itself identified as the sum of a number of points on several linguistic scales; defined by its place on several continua. Any utterance, however short, is susceptible of description with reference to a whole range of features. Michael Riffaterre ('Criteria for Style Analysis', *Word*, xv, [1959], p. 172) gives a good example from *Moby Dick:*

> And heaved and heaved, still unrestingly heaved the black sea, as if its vast tides were a conscience.

He comments:

> There is here an accumulation of (1) an unusual VS word-order; (2) the repetition of the verb; (3) the rhythm created by this ternary repetition (plus the combination of this phonetic device with the meaning: the rise and fall of the waves is 'depicted' by the rhythm); (4) the intensive co-ordination (*and . . . and . . .*), reinforcing the rhythm; (5) a nonce word (*unrestingly*) which by its very nature will create a surprise in any context; (6) the metaphor emphasized by the unusual relationship of the concrete (*tides*) to the abstract (*conscience*) instead of the reverse. Such a heaping up of stylistic features working together I should like to call *convergence.*

'Convergence' of stylistic features could of course be said to be present in any utterance; it is, in itself, nothing special. At any point in a text there is stratification of form; patterns at several levels working simultaneously. The style of a text is the totality of these patterns, especially patterns which are variables, not constants. We can compare styles as the sums of several stylistic features, taking each in turn as an individual feature for comparison.

So I have said that comparative stylistics consists of the comparison of texts in respect of one linguistic feature, or of a number of features taken separately. It can be imagined that a number of standard scales could be selected from the many that could be defined: say, scales based on those linguistic features which are known to be most variable—e.g. the frequency of segmental phonemes, which may be individual for separate poems, but not the order of morphemes in words, which is dictated as a constant in the language as a whole. Such standard criteria would obviously facilitate the process of whole-text stylistic comparison; but it is difficult to imagine that such a comparison, involving as it would the handling of so many variables, could be anything but extremely cumbersome. For the moment, we may prefer to restrict our stylistic comparisons to the evidence of one or a small number of linguistic features. Old English poetic texts could be compared in respect to the number of syllables per half-line; Ælfric's and Wulfstan's rhythmical styles could be compared by reference to the proportions of rhythm-units with internal alliteration. Seymour Chatman ('Comparing Metrical Styles' in Sebeok) has compared Pope's and Donne's versification by reference to quite a small area of metrics. *A Farewell to Arms* and *Finnegan's Wake* could be seen to occupy very different positions on various sub-level continua ranging from grammatical simplicity to complexity in the treatment of a number of constructions. Lyly and Browne could be compared in terms of the density of occurrence of certain lexical items (e.g. the names of mythological or legendary figures). It is evident that the linguistic discussion of style will be much dependent on frequencies of occurrence of variable linguistic features, and that, as has often been suggested, the results may conveniently be presented by statistical, or at least numerical, methods. But there will hardly be cases where a text is characterized as statistically deviant, in certain features, from an absolute norm which is the style of 'normal usage' quantified.

What sorts of linguistic features will be taken account of in 'linguistic stylistics'? Generally, only those which come within the level of form. Substance is of small interest: we are not concerned with the actual acoustics of speech-sounds, nor with the type used in printing a poem, except in very rare cases—for example, where written substance is organized to form an emblem which is presumably linked with formal features and contextual meaning; or where the sounds of part of a text are genuinely onomatopoeic—where substance is linked to context directly, and not through the usual channel of form. The other outside level, context, will be of constant interest to the linguist, though it will not be the object of his analysis. He must be conscious of the interaction of style and its contextual co-ordinate, register. And in the case of a literary text (by which I mean one that is commonly regarded as literary, rather than one that he has defined as literary), he can hardly free the text from the mass of contextual data that necessarily accumulates around it. He may be tempted to make connections between formal features and contextual observations—to discuss non-onomatopoeic sound-symbolism, for example—but such connexions will not be validated by his linguistic findings, and must remain, for the linguist, hypotheses.

Stylistic description in linguistic terms is the description of patterns at the level of form, specifically the identification of patterns formed by the arrangement of linguistic variables. Patterns occur at any of the three sub-levels, and are various within the sub-levels (so, in phonology, there may be patterns of syllables or of individual phonemes; in grammar, of clauses or of morphemes). Patterns may also be detected in inter-level relationships. The pattern *heaved . . . heaved . . . heaved* in Riffaterre's example from *Moby Dick* can be described as operating at each of the three sub-levels of form: at phonology, as the repetition of the sequence of phonemes /hiyvd/; at grammar, as the repetition of the grammatical unit V (past tense) (the same grammatical pattern would exist in *heaved . . . jumped . . . blessed*); at lexis, as the repetition of the lexical item *heaved*. Wulfstan's *Hy hergiað and hy bærnað, rypað and reafiað* has an insistent grammatical pattern, and a phonological pattern which differs from that of the *Moby Dick* sentence through involving repetition of stress-units (principally ′ ˣ), not phoneme-sequences. It has no remarkable lexical pattern, the lexical items being acceptably collocable. In each of these examples, the patterns of all sorts can be described as individual patterns, or in relation to other patterns at the same sub-level (as we might speak of the relation between alliteration and rhythm), or in relation to patterns at other sub-levels (statements of 'convergence'). If we are doing stylistic comparison, we are likely to take one type of pattern only, and note its occurrence in several texts; but single-text description normally requires relation of patterns to other patterns. Some texts cry out for description of convergence: e.g. Old English poetry, where there is a constant interplay of alliteration, stress-unit repetition, grammatical repetition, lexical variation; the couplet from Crabbe which Dr Rodway analyses; other short texts with a complex of concentrated, interrelating patterns, like

> Good is no good, but if it be spend:
> God giueth good for none other end.

from the *Shepheardes Calender*, and, from Shakespeare's Sonnet 43:

> All days are nights to see till I see thee,
> And nights bright days when dreams do show thee me.

It may be said that inter-level and intra-level linguistic analyses thrive on the complexity of this sort of poetry.

In this essay I have concentrated on the general issues surrounding the linguistic study of literature, attempting to make clear a linguist's attitude to his application of linguistic techniques to literary texts. He starts from the premise that literature has linguistic form, and determines to make no special assumptions for it before proceeding to analysis. There is, he argues, such an abstraction as 'the language as a whole', and it is his task to find out how certain examples of this language are characterized as distinct styles. His general linguistic theory has him believe that the area of language in which he studies linguistic variety is *form*, a category which excludes the physical substance of language and the contextual attributes surrounding it; even though context influences the selection of formal characteristics, he is not immediately concerned, in his analysis, with the 'why' of linguistic variety. General linguistic theory further subdivides the field of study: form is composed of phonology, grammar and lexis.

We could pass on from this position to the subject on which my chapter can have little to say: the details of linguistic analysis. A host of precise techniques is available for the minute study of form, a host constantly augmented as linguistics becomes more and more complicated. The whole range of linguistic terminology comes in. Apart from the variety in terminology—a result of the lack of agreement I mentioned at the beginning—there is a need for a multiplicity of terms and techniques. The formal structures of any language are so many and complex that they can be adequately reflected only by a complicated linguistics. Most schools of linguistics are well equipped to present the critic with a mass of data on the most recondite points: the frequency of phonemes, the exact stress-patterns in a metre, the clause-structure of a sonnet, lexical collocations in a lyric, distribution of Latinate words in an epic, and so on. But thoroughgoing linguistic exposition of the form of a text or texts is certain to be cumbersome and will perhaps be unpalatable. I am inclined to think that this grubbing out of facts is the least of the services of linguistics to the study of literature. Some of it may be invaluable in certain facets of literary history. But the difficulty of the exposition, the unfamiliarity and chaotic documentation of the method, will seem to inhibit immediacy of contact between critical mind and text. So I affirm above all the value of the attitudes and central concepts of linguistics: the insistence on description of form, the firm grasp of the parts of a linguistic act. Linguistics is just one form of training in close reading, and linguists—especially those whose studies have been in a language with a great literature—may be expected to be especially perceptive of the way language works in a literary text. Their training has also prepared them to be able to explain, in precise terms, the workings of language. As yet, linguistics employs a descriptive language very different from that of literary criticism, and we may expect some failures of communication when we talk about stylistic minutiae. But, stripped of its terminological ramifications, linguistics is a simple discipline. The simple framework of ideas may, we hope, pass from linguists to students of literature, to form *part* of the critical apparatus: a way of looking hard at a text itself, of separating text from non-text. It is, let it be repeated, to contribute to only a part of literary criticism: stylistic description, a department of criticism which has become more prominent in recent years. There is no logical step from linguistic criticism to evaluation or interpretation (except of points of detail); but linguistics does provide ways of unfolding and discussing precise textual effects, and may be a means of assuring a sound factual basis for many sorts of critical judgment.[8]

[8] For further discussion of the capacity and limitations of linguistics in literary studies, see Fowler, 'Linguistics, Stylistics; Criticism?' to appear in *Lingua* xvi (1966).

2

The New Criticism and the Language of Poetry

ONE OF THE basic assumptions of modern critical theory in England and America is that the literary work is essentially irreducible. Poetry, for those who hold the belief, is, indeed, itself and not another thing, and in no earlier time has the fabric of literature—the structure and texture of unique, autonomous wholes—assumed such importance for criticism as it does today. According to René Wellek an entire school of criticism can be characterized by the fact that it treats with full seriousness Mallarmé's platitude that poetry is made with words, not ideas. In the same essay Wellek notices a curious paradox deriving from recent methodological developments in literary criticism. After discussing the work of such linguists and critics as Trubetskoy, Vossler, Spitzer and Auerbach—writers whose work has revolutionized the study of European literatures—he contrasts the situation in the Anglo-Saxon world: 'Here the gulf between linguistics and literary criticism has widened deplorably. The critics are more and more ignorant of philology; and the linguists, especially the Yale school headed by the late Leonard Bloomfield, have expressly proclaimed their lack of interest in questions of style and poetic language. Interest in "language" is, however, prominent among British and American critics: but it is rather in "semantics", in the analysis of the role of "emotive" language contrasted with intellectual, scientific language. It is at the basis of the theories propounded by I. A. Richards.'[1]

Richards, in fact, in his most influential theoretical work, demonstrates not so much an ignorance of the techniques of philological analysis as a fear of their uncontrolled, mechanical application. Distinguishing the components of a critical statement as the *critical part*, or description of a literary experience, and the *technical part*, or description of the literary object, he felt it necessary to issue a vigorous warning against those who would actually substitute description of the object for judgment of the experience: 'The trick of judging the whole by the detail, instead of the other way about, of mistaking the means for the end, the technique for the value, is in fact much the most successful of the snares which waylay the critic. . . . We pay attention to externals when we do not know what else to do with a poem.'[2] One does not have to assent to the idea of technique as being somehow 'external' to share his misgivings of a critical programme proposing to itself the ideals of scientific description. On the other hand, to limit the area of joint operation between critics and linguists to the relatively specialized field of metrics and phonemics seems like the sad confession of an entrenched isolationalism.

The situation, in fact, is not really as bad as all that. There have been several works published in the last few years in which the concerns of linguistics and criticism have been combined in the study of a wide variety of formal aspects of literature. But if linguistic criticism, or critical linguistics, is going to affect the course of literary criticism in general, the change will not be brought about merely by critics seeking to repair their ignorance of philology, nor even by linguists adapting their analytic methods for the analysis of literary texts. These are desirable developments, of course, and through them criticism can gain immeasurably in clarity and precision. The really influential critics of our time, though, the ones responsible for the beginnings of a radical transformation of the entire scope of criticism, are just those whose interest in semantics has, according to Wellek,

[1] René Wellek, 'The Main Trends of Twentieth Century Criticism', *Concepts of Criticism*, ed. Stephen G. Nichols, Jr. (New Haven, 1963), p. 351.

[2] I. A. Richards, *Principles of Literary Criticism*, 4th ed. (New York, 1930), p. 24.

proved inimical to a desired development of criticism along European lines. Moreover, as long as linguists continue to pay only lip service to 'meaning', acknowledging its importance in footnotes but leaving any further exploration to the linguistic philosophers, the situation will remain the same. And in the event this may prove to be not at all deplorable. After all, linguists are the only ones properly qualified to determine the boundaries of their own subject satisfactorily, and the same applies to philosophy. From the critic's point of view at any rate, the most interesting progress has often been made on the common ground where their mutual, tentative exploration meets in such works as Willard von Orman Quine's *Word and Object* or Paul Ziff's *Semantic Analysis*. It is Quine, in fact, who insists upon their inseparability by citing James Grier Miller's terse dictum 'Ontology recapitulates philology'. And another philosopher, Philip Wheelwright, formulates a less cryptic, but not dissimilar proposition when he says: 'the Cartesian dualism of mind vs. matter, or in its latter forms subjective vs. objective, which has tended to give shape and direction to much of the philosophical thought since the seventeenth century, has begun to yield in many quarters to a three-fold thought structure, in which subject, object, and linguistic medium play irreducible and inter-causative roles in the formulation of what, for want of a better name, we may call reality'.[3] A recognition of these truths lies behind much of the single-minded preoccupation of modern critics with the language of literature, and ensures their continuing dependence upon the co-operation of both philosophers and linguists. What follows here is an attempt to examine the nature and the limits of this dependence and its consequences for practical criticism.

A belief in the centrality of linguistic media, or what are loosely defined as such, has resulted in the vastly increased importance accorded to symbolic logic by philosophers, myth by anthropologists and symbolism by Freudian psychologists. Animated by a similar conviction, the literary critics have been trying

[3] Philip Wheelwright, *Metaphor and Reality* (Bloomington, Indiana, 1962), p. 26.

for the last half-century, to isolate, if possible, the elements of a distinctive literary language. Success in this would, they felt, provide a key to open up literature to a new kind of critical enquiry, just as the advances in Freudian theory had unlocked the closed door of the individual psyche.

Claiming descent from Coleridge, the modern movement in critical theory took its direct inspiration at least from I. A. Richards. His is the classical statement of a view of poetic language which has been at the centre of critical controversy for forty years. In a justly famous chapter of his *Principles of Literary Criticism*, called 'The Two Uses of Language' he says:

> A statement may be used for the sake of the *reference*, true or false, which it causes. This is the *scientific* use of language. But it may also be used for the sake of the effects in emotion and attitude produced by the reference it occasions. This is the *emotive*. The distinction once clearly grasped is simple. We may either use words for the sake of the references they promote, or we may use them for the sake of the attitudes and emotions which ensue. Many arrangements of words evoke attitudes without any reference being required *en route*. They operate like musical phrases. But usually references are involved as *conditions* for, or *stages in*, the ensuing development of attitudes, yet it is still the attitudes not the references which are important. It matters not at all in such cases whether the references are true or false. Their sole function is to bring about and support the attitudes which are the further response. The questioning, verificatory way of handling them is irrelevant, and in a competent reader it is not allowed to interfere. (pp. 267–8)

The distinction he is making is, as he claims, a simple one, but its implications are complex and far reaching. The idea of poetry as the supreme form of emotive language commits one, for instance, to certain views about the psychology of reading. These ideas were explored in exhaustive detail, however, by Richards himself in the same book and need no rehearsal here. He also, more particularly in his later book *Practical Criticism*, examined more cursorily the consequences of the above distinction for the actual language of poetry, and this must be followed up because it led eventually to the critical theories associated with such people as Ransom, Brooks, Blackmur, Tate, Empson and Burke.

There are, Richards claimed, four points of view from which almost all articulate speech can be profitably regarded; those of sense, feeling, tone and intention. When we speak we do so in order to say something, but we also enunciate some feelings about the state of affairs we are referring to, and at the same time indicate an attitude towards a listener. Furthermore, when we speak we have some purpose for choosing to do so, and this purpose necessarily modifies our speech. It follows then, from what has been said before, that in poetry sense is almost always subordinated to feeling and tone. 'The poet makes a statement about something, not in order that the statement may be examined and reflected upon, but in order to evoke certain feelings, and when these are evoked the use of the statement is exhausted.'[4] This being the case, insistence upon a correspondence between statements in poetry and the facts to which they refer is futile, and often more than this, destructive of the poem's true value. When a poet seeks to attach a reader's attitudes which have arisen without dependence on a reference, but by the interplay and resolution of impulses aroused in other ways, to a certain belief, or set of beliefs, as Wordsworth does with his ideas about Pantheism, then he undermines the whole basis of his poem. Instead of sustaining the desired attitudes in his reader by the special means of poetry, linguistic and formal, he does so by trying to emulate the cognitive methods of science. Poetry again and again insists on its independence from what it actually says and Archibald MacLeish's poetic affirmation of this insight in *Ars poetica*, 'A poem should not mean/ But be', thus becomes an ingenious example of the Liar Paradox.

The kind of criticism which may be expected to result from these views is exemplified brilliantly though obliquely in *Practical Criticism* where Richards takes issue with students who had produced for him their own critical efforts. Concentrating on the expression and interaction of sense, feeling and tone in a number of short poems, he touches upon most of the major problems of modern criticism. His mind ranges widely over the entire

[4] I. A. Richards, *Practical Criticism* (New York, 1929), p. 354.

field of literary analysis, throwing light on such things as rhythm, metaphor, sentimentality, inhibition and meaning, as well as upon the related problems of irrelevant association and stock responses. At least until the advent of the Chicago critics, the major effort in English and American criticism has consisted of successive attempts to test the analytic tools he forged, on the body of English literature, or on parts of it.

Of all those critics and theorists who have disagreed with Richards about the nature of poetic discourse, while at the same time sharing his semantic approach to poetic language, the most influential is probably John Crowe Ransom, one of the founding members of the Fugitive group of poets and the foremost theoretician of the New Critics. Ransom's theory, which also finds strong echoes in the writings of Allen Tate and Robert Penn Warren, is rooted in his dissatisfaction with Richards's attempt to discriminate prose and poetic discourse. Feeling that poetry, when identified only by its capacity to tease dormant affective states into unusual activity, becomes somewhat disreputable, Ransom finds a more promising differentia in the kind of structure exemplified by a poem. In its simplest form that structure can be defined as 'a loose logical structure with an irrelevant local texture'.[5] Over a period of time Ransom has elaborated this definition, and has linked his theory of poetry to a Metaphysic and an Epistemology, but its consequences for criticism can be adequately studied just by looking at his own informed account of the difficulties of composing poems on what he calls 'the two-ground basis of (1) an intended meaning and (2) an intended meter', an operation in which the argument of the poem fights to displace the metre and the metre fights to displace the argument. What interests Ransom most is the nature of the compromise necessitated by the fact that to receive a metre at all an argument cannot be perfectly logical but must admit some indeterminacy of meaning, and that likewise a metrical form must also be partly indeterminate in order to embody an argument.

The diagram reproduced below is Ransom's way of describing the process of poetic composition:

[5] John Crowe Ransom, *The New Criticism* (Norfolk, Connecticut), p. 280.

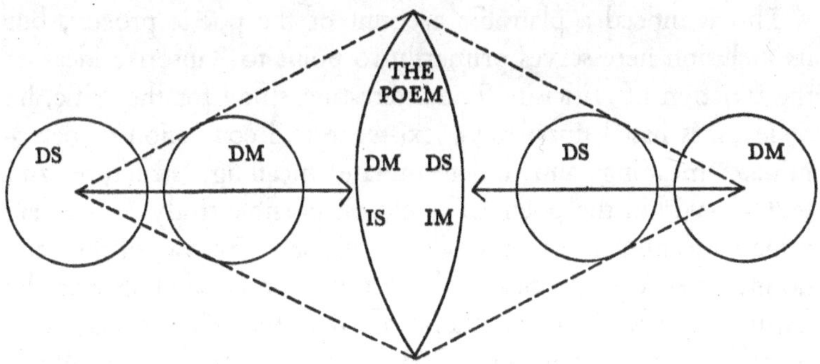

D.S. is Determinate Sound or the metre.

I.S. is Indeterminate Sound or the phonetic character the sounds have assumed which is in no relation to the metre.

D.M. is the Determinate Meaning or logical paraphrase of the poem.

I.M. is the Indeterminate Meaning or that part of the meaning which took shape not according to its own logical necessity but under metrical compulsion.

And this is a summary of his account in *The New Criticism* of what is actually happening in the diagram:

> In theory, the poem is the resultant of two processes coming from opposite directions. Starting from the left of the diagram the poet is especially concerned with his metre, D.S., which may be blocked out in a series of accented and unaccented syllables arranged in lines, possibly even with rhyme endings; but there is also D.M., a prose discourse which has to be reduced to the phonetic pattern of the metre; the poet's inclination at this stage is to replace its words with others which suit the metre but which convey the meaning less exactly. But he is checked by the converse process, in which he has to make a metre for his prose meaning and the temptation is to replace the required metrical sounds with others that suit his logic and are not quite so good for the metre. When all the adaptations have been made we are left with a poem in which the arc at the left represents the liberties meaning has taken with metre, and the one at the right, the liberties taken by metre with meaning.

This is indeed a plausible account of the poetic process, but its inclusion here serves primarily to point to Ransom's ideas of the function of criticism. The interesting study for the critic, he believes, is based upon the coexistence and connexion of determinate meaning and indeterminate meaning, structure and texture, within the poem. The closest possible study of indeterminate meaning as it is smuggled into poetry by way of the back door of metrical necessity might throw a good deal of light on the nature of poetic discourse. Ransom's own studies in the relation of metre and meaning in the poetry of Wordsworth, Pope, Milton and Marvell, fragmentary though they are, suggest the degree of importance he would allow to linguistics in literary criticism.

A more radical critique of Richards's theory of emotive/descriptive language has been made in a recent book by Isabel Hungerland. Mrs Hungerland appears to be cutting at the very roots of previous discussion when she declares, after subjecting four short poetic extracts to different forms of analysis from those recommended by Richards, that 'there is no such thing as a poetic language either as a diction or as a mode of sentential meanings. . . . All the modes of meaning, features and functions of everyday language are found in poetry. In brief, the medium of poetry is living language.'[6] It may be doubted whether the criticism of Richards's emotive/descriptive distinction upon which this declaration is based is a sound one, though this is not to say, of course, that her own theoretical position is also necessarily unsound. Such an 'ordinary language' view of literature certainly has many adherents, and its relevance to our general discussion of linguistics and criticism is apparent.

Mrs Hungerland sets out to examine the concept of tone in poetry by analysing grammatically, the four following excerpts:

> If there be rags enough, he will know her name
> And be well pleased remembering it, for in the old days,
> Though she had young men's praise and old men's blame,
> Among the poor both old and young gave her praise.
>
> (W. B. YEATS, *Her Praise*)

[6] Isabel Hungerland, *Poetic Discourse*, University of California Publications in Philosophy, vol. 33 (Berkeley and Los Angeles, 1958), pp. 13–43.

She walks in beauty, like the night
Of cloudless climes and starry skies;
And all that's best of dark and bright
Meet in her aspect and her eyes:
Thus mellow'd to that tender light
Which heaven to gaudy day denies.

(BYRON, *She Walks in Beauty*)

She lived unknown, and few could know
When Lucy ceased to be;
But she is in her grave, and oh,
The difference to me!

(WORDSWORTH, *Lucy ii*)

Let us roll all our strength and all
Our sweetness up into one ball,
And tear our pleasures with rough strife
Thorough the iron gates of life:

(MARVELL, *To his Coy Mistress*)

The tonal variation she finds here, moving from the restraint of Yeats's lines through the growing urgency in Byron and Marvell, to the final intensity of Wordsworth's stanza, appears to depend partly, she thinks, on the kind of sentence each poet uses. Yeats employs a subjunctive hypothetical and a statement of evidence for it; Byron's sentences have commendation words in their predicates and subjects; Wordsworth moves to an exclamation, and Marvell uses a polite form of the imperative. It is at this point in her analysis that she begins to beg the question by remarking that the type of sentence used in Yeats's poem is one belonging to the family of expressions characteristic of scientific discourse. This fact is, she supposes, enough to dispose of the emotive language theory altogether, though it is difficult to see how this line of thought relates logically to Richards's at all. However, this is the conclusion built upon the preceding analysis:

> The descriptive-emotive dichotomy, it should now be clear, does not make a useful cut through language. For example, in trying to classify the excerpts from four poems on this basis, we seem

> at first to get Yeats on one side, with descriptive meaning, and the other three, lumped together across the divide, with emotive meaning. On the other hand, since Yeats's 'description' would ordinarily arouse some feelings in the reader, Yeats's lines apparently have both kinds of meaning. Also, since the other excerpts contain what the theory calls 'descriptive words', they cannot be purely emotive in meaning. We end, then, with the unenlightening conclusion that all four excerpts have both kinds of meaning. This does not help us to understand certain tonal differences between one excerpt and the others.

By taking this line of reasoning she has, however, come close to Ransom's position. The similarity is even more marked in a later passage where she puts forward her own views on the difference between the language of science and that of literature: 'Both literary discourse and scientific discourse are specializations of everyday discourse.... Science tends to specialize, linguistically, by excluding certain everyday forms and functions and inventing its own vocabulary. Literature has no tendency towards a clearly technical diction. It specializes, one might say, by making common forms of language function more effectively than they do in ordinary discourse, but in ways that are not at all foreign to ordinary life' (p. 46).

Mrs Hungerland goes on to work out the implications of her 'ordinary language' theory in respect of figurative language and symbolism, but this detailed working out of its implications we may ignore. The point to be made is that in spite of her contrary claims, *Poetic Discourse* does not represent a departure from the main line of modern critical doctrine so much as a further refinement of it. It is significant that she is unable to dismiss completely the claims of those who find ambiguity, paradox and irony essential to poetic discourse, but admits the view as a half-truth. Again it is doubtful whether she is attacking any real adversaries here, though the vague phrase 'half-truth' makes it difficult to tell. Ransom, it will be recalled, without specifying any particular kinds of indeterminate meaning, thought that a study of such textural devices—and it is clear from his examples that he would certainly include ambiguity, paradox and irony, as well as any others that happen to be there—might lead the critic most easily to the heart of the poem. Of course, to say this does not rule out the importance of determinate meaning in literature, as well as what he calls determinate and indeterminate sound. Mrs Hungerland's theory of poetry, like the others we have examined, rests upon a belief that the way to a poem is through its language. The relative homogeneity of all these theories can best be observed by setting them against a thoroughly unsympathetic doctrine which sees New Criticism as merely another version of the Hellenistic-Roman subjection of poetics to grammar and rhetoric. This description is R. S. Crane's, the acknowledged leader of the school of theorists best described in Kenneth Burke's phrase, the Chicago Neo-Aristotelians. In an attempt to avoid what they thought of as an undesirable Platonism in the works of the New Critics, a tendency to *a priori* thinking about the problems of poetry, the Chicago critics attempted to substitute an inductive, pluralistic approach to the criticism of literature in which critical procedures for individual works would be dictated solely by the demands of the work itself. Their adherence to Aristotelian principles, however, has tended to result in the substitution of one dogma for another, one form of critical monism being supplanted by another in which the work of art is defined in relation to its various causes, final, formal, efficient and material. It is not a purpose of this essay to offer a critique of the doctrines of the Chicago school, however, but to indicate here the existence of a theory in which language, the material cause of a literary work, is seen as just one of several factors in its creation, and by no means the most important, as is evident in Elder Olson's essay from which the following is taken:

> Nowadays when the nature of poetry has become so uncertain that everyone is trying to define it, definitions usually begin: 'poetry is words which, or language which, or discourse which,' and so forth. As a matter of fact, it is nothing of the kind. Just as we should not define a chair as wood which has such and such characteristics—for a chair is not a kind of wood but furniture—so we ought not to define poetry as a kind of language. The chair is not

> wood but wooden; poetry is not words but verbal. In one sense, of course, the words are of the utmost importance; if they are not the right words or if we do not grasp them, we do not grasp the poem. In another sense, they are the least important elements in the poem, for they do not determine the character of anything else in the poem; on the contrary, they are determined by everything else. They are the only things we see or hear; yet they are governed by imperceptible things which are inferred from them. And when we are moved by poetry, we are not moved by the words, except in so far as sounds and rhythms move us; we are moved by the things that the words stand for.[7]

As one might expect, linguistic analysis plays a relatively minor role in the work of the Neo-Aristotelians, much more emphasis being placed on the examination of such large elements of structure as plot, and on the relation of part to part and part to whole.

The next logical step in any account of the development of New Criticism should involve a comprehensive explanation of how the concepts already discussed—tone and feeling, texture or indeterminate meaning and sound, and the specialization of ordinary language—have been interpreted by various critics. But because these derivative critical systems have been adequately explored in greater detail than could be attempted here by, among others, Edgar Hyman, Murray Kreiger, William Righter and Richard Foster,[8] it is proposed to restrict any further abstract discussion to the minimum compatible with intelligibility, before going on to see how such theories have fared in actual critical practice.

One of the most succinct attempts to relate Richards's psychology of reading to the specific linguistic devices used in poetry, was that made by Cleanth Brooks in *Modern Poetry and the Tradition*, and later in *The Well Wrought Urn*. Brooks saw that, if the effect of poetry is to resolve and reconcile attitudes within the

[7] Elder Olson, 'An Outline of Poetic Theory', *Critics and Criticism*, ed. R. S. Crane (Chicago, 1957), p. 21, n. 8.

[8] Edgar Hyman, *The Armed Vision* (New York, 1947); Murray Krieger, *The New Apologists for Poetry* (Minneapolis, 1956); William Righter, *Logic and Criticism* (London, 1963); Richard Foster, *The New Romantics: A Reappraisal of the New Criticism* (Bloomington, Indiana, 1962).

reader, then poems could be ranged in a hierarchy of value according to the complexity and variety of the attitudes involved, and more interestingly, could be studied in terms of the specific techniques used in the poem's attempt to resolve those apparently antithetical attitudes. Thus in his own criticism a great deal of emphasis is placed upon paradox, 'a device for contrasting the conventional views of a situation, or the limited and special view of it, such as those taken in practical and scientific discourse, with a more inclusive view'; wit, or 'awareness of the multiplicity of possible attitudes to be taken toward a given situation'; and irony, 'a device for definition of attitudes by qualification'.[9] To these, he might have added a fourth, allied term, ambiguity, the complex applications of which had already been explored by Empson in his earlier book, *Seven Types of Ambiguity*. He does use the concept, in fact, along with paradox, wit and irony, in the course of analysing poems by Milton, Pope, Wordsworth, Keats, Gray, Tennyson and Yeats.

Two other attempts to isolate the special properties of poetry have produced the closely related concepts of 'gesture', and 'symbolic action'. The first of these is formulated by R. P. Blackmur in his book, *Language as Gesture*, and the other is discussed intermittently by Kenneth Burke throughout his book, *A Grammar of Motives*. For our present purpose it will be enough to glance at Blackmur's explanation of 'gesture'; we shall have to come to grips with Burke's views in another part of this essay anyway. Gesture in language, says Blackmur, is the meaningfulness which is moving in every sense of the word. It helps to move the words as it helps to move the reader. It is the 'play of meaningfulness among words which cannot be defined in the formulas of the dictionary, but which is defined in their use together'.[10] The resemblance of this to the earlier definitions quoted will be obvious. What is especially interesting about his theory though, is the way in which it is used to demonstrate how elements of determinate sound are specifically connected with elements of indeterminate meaning, as, for example, in his

[9] Cleanth Brooks, *The Well Wrought Urn* (New York, 1947), p. 230.
[10] R. P. Blackmur, *Language as Gesture* (New York, 1952), p. 6.

discussions of metre, punctuation, rhyme and refrain. In an essay on the poetic technique of Marianne Moore, he digresses briefly about his methods. He is, he says, selecting the formal aspects of the poem which are most readily demonstrable, things like rhyme, pattern and punctuation, from which he can reach further into its technical nature, the conventional or general meanings of the words arranged by form. The only vindication he would claim for his procedure is that it works; experience shows that by selective analysis of the relation of part to part within the poem, the critic becomes aware of what the particular tensions produce. Whilst the importance of relating elements of sound and meaning will readily be granted by critics sharing a bias in favour of linguistic criticism, Blackmur's highly selective techniques must be anathema to the thorough-going positivist. Indeed, it is probably on this issue more than any other that the linguist parts company with the critic.

The last theory of poetic language we shall need to look at is Allen Tate's. In an essay called 'Tension in Poetry', he makes this term, 'tension', stand for all the extension and intension, denotation and connotation, that can be discovered in a poem. Taking Ransom's ideal nearer to its logical conclusion, Tate says that: 'The remotest figurative significance that we can derive does not invalidate the extensions of the literal statement. Or we may begin with the literal statement and by stages develop the complications of metaphor: at every stage we may pause to state the meaning so far apprehended, and at every stage the meaning will be coherent.'[11] The two contrasted methods of approach are then discovered to have particular application to contrasted kinds of poetry. The metaphysical or rationalist poet takes as his starting point, if not a literal statement, then something approximating to one, and from it develops its intension as far as he can in an effort to occupy the whole scale of meaning. The romantic or symbolist poet works in the opposite direction, searching for rational statements to embody his unattached connotations. In the best poetry, however, which Tate calls 'poetry of the centre', tension is achieved when the

[11] Allen Tate, *Collected Essays* (Denver, 1959), p. 83.

particular strategy employed is fully diffused in the attainment of a unitary effect.

This theory raises, and makes no effort to solve, difficult problems about the psychology of composition, and the relation of connotation to denotation. It does, however, hint at an answer to the charge that New Criticism is only equipped to deal with certain limited kinds of poetry, though the only really convincing refutation of such an accusation would be not theoretical but practical. At this point, therefore, it should prove instructive to examine some of the best criticism, representative of the theories we have considered, and compare it with that of critics subscribing to different critical philosophies.

The best way of conducting such an examination would be, perhaps, to assemble a number of critiques of a given work to form a kind of critical spectrum, showing at one end of its range various kinds of 'contextualist' criticisms, in which the authors explain the work in terms of its origins or effects, and at its other extreme, non-selective statistical analyses of the linguistic features of the same text. Somewhere in between these positions we should find the majority of critical opinions, differentiated by the greater or lesser importance allowed to form (phonological, grammatical or syntactical), meaning and context. Unfortunately the interesting contrasts afforded by such a juxtaposition are denied us by reason of the fact that no single work has attracted the attention of a sufficient variety of critics. It is possible though, to do something of the kind by enlarging the area of our interest to include a fairly homogeneous body of work by a single author, and by settling for a limited number of representative critical viewpoints. Keats's shorter poems, in particular his sonnets and odes, have received enough attention from a sufficiently disparate group of commentators to serve this purpose. Moreover, as we have remarked, the New Critics have often been charged with a failure to apply their techniques successfully to Romantic lyric poetry, so the choice of Keats should be doubly revealing.

In the hope of showing how a poem's phonemic totality supports and contributes to its prose and poetic statement, J. J. Lynch, in an article called 'The Tonality of Lyric Poetry: An Experiment in Method',[12] has analysed the sound patterns of Keats's sonnet *On First Looking into Chapman's Homer.* From this analysis, in which all the poem's sounds were given values in accordance with a predetermined system, he concludes that the word 'silent', which for reasons briefly outlined, is said to sum up or climax the poem's theme, also sums up the phonemic structure of the sonnet. Attempting to arrive at some more general conclusions about the relation of sound and meaning in lyric poems, Dell H. Hymes went on from this to analyse twenty sonnets, ten each by Wordsworth and Keats, and here too it was discovered that in a significant proportion of them a particular word which came near the end of the poem and was judged to sum up its theme also embodied its dominant sound pattern.

Assuming that these analytic procedures have been satisfactorily evolved and properly administered, one is then left with Hymes's claim that the technique can help in directing the reader to the source of a lyric poem's essential organization. He thinks that a complete account of the phonemic patterns avoids the dangers of a purely intuitive linguistic approach, as exemplified by the work of Leo Spitzer, just as the stringent application of three criteria for the existence of a summative word escapes the limitations of the statistical method, which often, in its scientific zeal, appears to ignore the fact that it is dealing with an aesthetic object.

This kind of critical analysis could obviously lend a needed rigour to the existing techniques of modern criticism, helping to discriminate the elements of determinate and indeterminate sound in a poem, and showing just how they function there. It is open to question, though, whether the authors of this theory do in fact steer so cleanly as they would like to think between the twin rocks of intuition and objectivity. Towards the end of his paper, Hymes, turning for confirmation of his findings to other poems says that: 'Analysis of a poem of my own revealed an organization I had not suspected. The final word "ministry" summed up the dominant phonemes, and, as it turned out, provided a key to the poem's four stanzas, each of which *could be seen*

[12] In *Word*, ix (1953).

as expressing a form of ministry.'[13] (My italics.) Once the control represented by independent analysis of meaning and form is relaxed, the way is left open for any kind of contrived interpretation. In the same way, manipulation of different systems of phonological analysis could doubtless be made to produce confirmation of one's analysis of a poem's meaning. Indeed, it is difficult to see how a single word which summarizes the theme of the poem *can* be arrived at independently of other considerations, except in a few obvious instances. It is significant, perhaps, that one of the reasons Lynch gives for choosing the word 'silent' in Keats's poem is that it occupies a crucial position in the poem's metrical design. Thus he too appears to be falling into the trap of assuming part of what he sets out to prove: that a word which plays a summative role in the meaning of a poem might also prove to occupy a similar position in its pattern of sound.

Furthermore, the results of this kind of analysis seem to be, if not vitiated, then at least rendered less valuable by the limitations the authors voluntarily impose upon themselves. Following Benjamin Bailey's assertion that Keats had a theory of melody which held that vowels should be managed so as not to clash with each other, a great deal of work has been carried out by various people in connexion with the assonantal patterning of Keats's verse. Walter Jackson Bate, for example, shows in his book on Keats's stylistic development, how lines of poetry were revised for the sake of achieving different distributions of vowel sounds; in this particular sonnet the line:

> Yet could I never judge what Men could mean

becoming in the final version:

> Yet did I never breathe its pure serene;[14]

The usefulness of a technique which is not flexible enough to be adapted in the light of this kind of evidence might be very limited.

A different kind of linguistic approach is represented in the

[13] Dell H. Hymes, 'Phonological Aspects of Style: Some English Sonnets', *Style in Language*, ed. Thomas A. Sebeok (Cambridge, Mass., 1960), p. 127.

[14] Walter Jackson Bate, *The Stylistic Development of Keats* (New York, 1945), p. 57.

work of two critics who rebel against what one of them calls the 'anti-intellectualism' of the New Critics.[15] The other, Leo Spitzer, in a footnote to one of his essays on three Middle English poems, outlines his well-known methods: 'My procedure involves two separate movements (both of which, taken together, serve to complete the "philological circle"): I first draw from one detail (which need not always be linguistic or stylistic, but may also be compositional in nature) of incontrovertible factual evidence, an inference as to the (at this stage still hypothetic) psyche of the author or the period, which hypothesis is then, in a second movement, controlled by a scrutiny of (to the degree that this is feasible) *all* other striking details (stylistic or compositional) which occur in the same author or period.'[16]

In Spitzer's essay on the *Ode on a Grecian Urn*,[17] this method is unfortunately somewhat obscured by his aim of refuting Wasserman's reading of the same poem. At the same time that he welcomes Wasserman's general approach to poetry, whereby a philological analysis is supplemented by researches in the history of ideas, so that the intellectual structures existing behind the sensuous experiences are brought to light, Spitzer feels that Wasserman has gone too far in making the text appear more intricate than it truly is, and, in doing so, has out-metaphysicized the poem.

In point of fact, Wasserman begins his long analysis of the ode in *The Finer Tone* by announcing his belief that the poem must be treated not as an abstract statement or an excursion into philosophy, but as a poem about 'things', which, he says, have a separate logic of their own, a meta-grammar of poetic imagery. He seems at this point to be reaffirming Allen Tate's view that Romantic poetry depends more for its meaning on the intension of words than on their extension. And he goes on to isolate clusters of images and to examine what he calls their syntax. Behind this apparent New Critical orthodoxy, however, are

[15] Earl R. Wasserman, *The Finer Tone: Keats' Major Poems* (Baltimore, 1953), p. 3.

[16] Leo Spitzer, 'Three Great Middle English Poems', *Essays on English and American Literature* (Princeton, 1962), p. 194.

[17] Leo Spitzer, 'The "Ode on a Grecian Urn", or Content vs. Metagrammar', *Essays on English and American Literature*, pp. 67–97.

some rather unusual controlling assumptions about how a poem expresses its meaning. No one, Wasserman says, will deny that the ode, like most of Keats's poems, deals with the human and the mutable on the one hand, and the immortal and essential on the other; and that what it states has something to do with an opposition and fusion of the two modes. Assent to this innocuous sounding general proposition is then taken to commit the reader to an entire Keatsian cosmology in which everything is dominated by this paradoxical collocation of contraries and their mystic interfusion. Having found in the 'mystic oxymoron' a key to Keats's poetic universe, he wields it with obsessive determination to unlock the linguistic complexities of the poem, bending the ode's verbal design to the shape of his original intuition.

Thus, though he does isolate certain important images, he carefully selects those which help to confirm his thesis. Similarly, he analyses the rhythms of parts of selected stanzas and claims to have demonstrated a viable connexion between the poem's sound and sense. Finally, he discovers a scale of grammatical moods in some of Keats's sentences, arranged, he says, in order of increasingly empathic relationships between subject and predicate. Spitzer has little difficulty in showing how unsound such an idea is, though what is more disturbing than any individual error of judgment is the critical method itself in which selected philological detail is used as evidence in support of intuitions about the nature of Keats's thought.

Spitzer himself begins his critique of the ode by placing it in its correct literary genre, *ekphrasis*, or the description of a pictorial or sculptural work of art. Is this, then, the compositional detail, if it can be called that, of incontrovertible factual evidence upon which Spitzer's reading is based? Or is the repetition of the word 'or' in the first stanza, with all that the word implies about Keats's failure to understand the historical scenes depicted on the urn, the significant linguistic detail? This is not made clear by any subsequent analysis, though the reading suggested by the latter detail would seem to be the more fruitful one, leading to an interpretation which sees the poem as a movement from intense but futile speculation about the nature of the three pastoral scenes on the urn, to the poet's spiritual relief obtained by his sudden perception of the beauty of the whole work of art. Though the archeological or historical information may have been lost, the aesthetic message is still alive and clear.

The importance of this interpretation comes out most clearly at the crux of Spitzer's argument with Wasserman, where he discusses the lines which have assumed such great importance in nearly all critical discussion of the poem:

> 'Beauty is truth, truth beauty',—that is all
> Ye know on earth, and all ye need to know.

Wasserman believes that the words 'that is all Ye know on earth, and all ye need to know' are spoken by the poet to Mankind, and that the word 'that' refers not merely to the preceding aphorism, but to the lines:

> When old age shall this generation waste,
> Thou [the urn] shall remain, in midst of other woes
> Than ours, a friend to man, to whom thou say'st
> 'Beauty is truth, truth beauty'...

He gives two reasons for his view. First, he says that it cannot be the urn which is telling man that all he knows on earth is that beauty is truth, because this is obviously not the case. He knows other things besides this. Presumably, this is what Quiller Couch, who did not question that Keats was here talking to Man, meant when he called it an 'uneducated conclusion', though one pardonable in so young a man. In the second place, this message, if delivered by the urn, has not been acted out at all in the rest of the poem. Now Spitzer's view is, of course, that this is just what the rest of the poem *is* saying: that the Platonic equation, beauty is truth, is alone precious knowledge in contrast to all forms of historical erudition. What is interesting is that to establish this meaning Spitzer believes that it is not at all necessary to examine the poem's imagery, or indeed any aspect of its indeterminate meaning or sound. If any general point can be deduced from Spitzer's methods in this essay, it is the one he states clearly himself: 'To establish an imagistic metagrammar which would ignore the all-controlling "intellectual grammar" of a poem would be to set in motion a dangerous "sorcerer's apprentice". Let us have, in our explanations of the classical poems of English literature, less of imagistic magic or alchemy that smells of the lamp, and more of that open air of crystalline lucidity around the work of art—as this is present in Keats's ode, in which thought and image have become naturally one because image has not encroached on thought, because thought has found its appropriate embodiment.'

Somewhere between the extremes of statistical linguistics and intuitive philology, most of the writings of the New Critics can be located. Their major effort in respect of Keats's odes, as we might expect, has been directed to an explanation of the relation between logical structure and local texture, philosophical aphorisms and their embodiment in pictorial images.

Allen Tate has argued, consistently with his theoretical position outlined above, that the last stanza of the *Ode on a Grecian Urn* is 'an illicit commentary added by the poet to a "meaning" which was symbolically complete at the end of the preceding stanza'.[18] Like Tate, W. K. Wimsatt believes that in the best Romantic poetry the tenor and vehicle of metaphor are wrought by parallel processes out of the same material. Writing about 'The Structure of Romantic Nature Imagery'[19] Wimsatt compares Coleridge's sonnet *To the River Otter* with a poem by Bowles having a very similar theme, and accounts for the superiority of the former poem by the fact that in it, the river landscape is both the occasion of the reminiscences which form the subject of the poem, and the source of the metaphor by which the reminiscences are described. Keats's poem has a similar coherence throughout four of its stanzas, which it then relinquishes in the fifth for the sake of an abstract commentary.

Kenneth Burke, who appears to agree with this theoretical position, interprets the ode as a poem about the two poles of knowledge symbolized by the language of art and the language of

[18] Allen Tate, 'A Reading of Keats', *Collected Essays*, p. 179.
[19] In *The Verbal Icon* (New York, 1962), pp. 103–16.

science, and therefore fully justified in moving by a series of transformations to the philosophical proposition, beauty is truth. Burke's subtle reading of the poem, so typical in its methods of much New Criticism, is worth following in detail.[20]

For Burke, a poem is a symbolic act, which, in its survival as a structure, enables the reader to re-enact the poet's original deed. The language of poetry, unlike the language of science, is to be considered not epistemologically, but symbolically. Thus, in a special sense, his reading of the poem is a symbolic one. Without belabouring the concept, Burke also uses the rhetorical term 'mystic oxymoron' to point to a central paradox in the poem; the idea of the *eternal present*, imaged in terms of unheard sounds, stilled motion and arrested pre-ecstasy. Then moving briefly outside the poem ('linguistic analysis has opened up new possibilities in the correlating of producer and product—and these concerns have such important bearing upon matters of culture and conduct in general that no sheer conventions or ideals of criticism should be allowed to interfere with their development' —*A Grammar of Motives*, p. 451) he attempts to make a connexion between Keats's illness and art, and the general fact that Romanticism with its stress on creativeness leads to the possibility of bodily suffering redeemed by a poetic act. This division into two contrasted realms of spiritual action and sensual passion is made fully manifest in the third, crucial stanza:

> All breathing human passion far above,
> That leaves a heart high-sorrowful and cloy'd,
> A burning forehead, and a parching tongue.

At this point the poem moves off in a new direction. Originally the bodily passion served as the scene or ground of the spiritual action, but at the end of stanza three, the level of bodily passion is abandoned by the spiritual or transcendent action, which now would seem to require a scene of the same quality as itself in which it can be properly embodied. This is provided by the scene in the fourth stanza where the imagery—sacrifice, piety,

[20] Kenneth Burke, 'Symbolic Action in a Poem by Keats,' *A Grammar of Motives and a Rhetoric of Motives* (Cleveland and New York, 1962).

silence, desolation—is that of communication with the immortal or the dead. Burke goes on to show how this stanza, which he likens to the sestet of a sonnet, is tonally related, by reason of its rhetorical questions, to the earlier part of the poem. This second movement of the poem reaches its climax in the words 'Cold Pastoral', which exemplify the benign, transcendental chill with which the poem ends. Thus, dramatistically, the poem enacts the propositon to which it finally gives explicit, conceptual expression; the terms 'beauty' and 'truth' being in some sense equivalents for 'poetry' or 'act,' and 'science' or 'scene'.

Like Burke's dramatistic analysis of the ode's imagery, Cleanth Brooks's reading of the poem is predominantly semantic in its bias. It is directed primarily to demonstrating that the elements of meaning which older critics—Garrod for instance—had thought to be out of Keats's control, form, in fact, a substructure of irony and paradox, culminating in the phrase to which Burke also draws attention, 'Cold Pastoral': 'The word "pastoral" suggests warmth, spontaneity, the natural and the informal as well as the idyllic, the simple, and the informally charming . . . but the "sylvan historian" works in terms of marble. The urn itself is cold, and the life beyond life which it expresses is life which has been formed, arranged.'[21] (It would be interesting to know whether this phrase, which is made to carry so great a weight of meaning, and which is also so striking from a phonological and a metrical point of view, is also 'summative' when analysed in relation to the ode's overall sound pattern.)

Brooks does not claim to have produced a novel interpretation of the *Ode on a Grecian Urn*, but to have shown how the philosophical 'bit of wisdom' is derived from its poetic context. And this, it is fair to say, has been the chief contribution of those critics who have pursued the methods, more or less rigorously, of New Criticism, to show that in the unique, unstable configurations of poetic discourse, meaning is constantly redetermined by use. None of the above descriptions of the ways in which a poem expresses its meaning is completely adequate; but taken together they do help to define the area in which critical progress is most

[21] Cleanth Brooks, *The Well Wrought Urn*, p. 150.

likely to be made. And it is here that linguistics could really revolutionize criticism, by helping to explicate the more obscure relations in literature, between structure and texture, sound and meaning, scene and act.

The influence of nineteenth-century philological scholarship is still strong in criticism, and will no doubt continue to be so. For those who believe that in the last line and a half of the *Ode on a Grecian Urn*, the poet is talking to the urn itself, no amount of linguistic analysis of the poem's sound patterns is going to displace their faith in the scanty evidence of Keats's occasional, aberrant use of the word 'ye' in the singular person.[22] And even if these attempts to bolster up intuition with dubious factual support are badly conceived, the scepticism which inspires them, doubting of the efficacy of the more mechanical forms of positivistic analysis, is surely justified. Critical achievements, like those in science, are always dependent upon the quality of an initial hypothesis. Here as elsewhere, in the first analysis, there is no substitute for sense.

[22] See Martin Halpern, 'Keats's Grecian Urn and the Singular "Ye"', *College English*, xxiv (1963), and also correspondence in *T.L.S.* (February, March 1964).

3

By Algebra to Augustanism

THIS IS AN AGE of criticism, so much an age of criticism that in certain quarters—particularly in the U.S.A.—literature is regarded as a more primitive form which justifies its existence only by providing raw material for processing. Certainly, students of literature nowadays prefer reading criticism, for the critic displays in full-flowering clarity what was perhaps buried or obscure in the rich confusion of the original work. He relates that work to Man and Morality, to Nature and Science, to History and Society, he sees its analogues and antecedents, and foresees its descendants and its role in worldmaking. Moreover, he marshals the Many into One system. No wonder, then, in such transcendence, he should seem preferable.

One snag, of course, is that *good* critics are much scarcer than good creative writers. But one has only to mention the first few names that spring to mind—Leavis, Empson, Ransom, Brooks—to be forced to acknowledge that the New Criticism has scored great successes. The more surprising, then, to find this well-armed task force (whose weapons and victories are respectively recorded in Hyman's volumes *The Armed Vision* and *The Critical Performance*[1]) apparently powerless to deal with a major continent of the literary world. Or is it? The techniques employed serve admirably for Romantic, Symbolist or Metaphysical poetry or novels, for work that is complex and obscure or mystical and

[1] Vintage Books, New York, 1955, 1956.

intuitive. This is partly because these works are the ones that have received most attention; they offered plenty of matter for teaching and none of the taught could suppose they were merely being given what they could see for themselves. However, the main reason for success is surely that the techniques were designed to refer the unclear poem to other areas of discourse which might throw a light on it. Strictly speaking, they are metacritical: the work is taken to be a symbolic or metaphorical expression of what could be expressed more directly in ethical, economic, psychological or metaphysical terms. Even Empson's close semantic analysis was directed to the elucidation of psychological ambiguities.

In short, the difficult New Criticism seems to have been a proper and useful response to the challenge of the difficult, new literature of the twentieth century. To put it crudely, such criticism can make exciting sense of poems which would seem absurd if taken literally in this age of science and analysis. This is done by *using* analysis and science (particularly psychology, sociology and anthropology) to show that such works make sense if taken obliquely. Since the modes in question are typically metaphorical modes of poetry, such notions as 'levels of meaning', 'complexity', 'ambiguity', 'condensation', 'displacement', 'ritual', 'emblem', 'symbol', 'gesture', 'gestalt', 'economy', 'inflation', 'rite', 'archetype', 'visceral', 'enacting', 'participation', and so forth can all prove useful. They can show that the meaning is more than the sum of separate statements, that what seems to be a bad argument is offered as a good experience, or a mode of ritual activity. But what of poetry which is neither obscure nor mystical, whose meaning *is* more or less contained in its statements, whose 'levels of meaning' are usually no more than one: that of the surface? What of the poetry of Good Sense?

On Augustan work, modern critics have operated not like eighteenth-century critics but like eighteenth-century surgeons: painfully, with the wrong tools; most successfully where the work happened to be uncharacteristically ambiguous or visceral, least successfully in terms of its Background or Thought. Many such poems could be dealt with in terms of general structure, as Warburton dealt with Pope. But such study of the relationship of parts to each other and to the whole has not much commended itself—naturally enough perhaps, for the critic of post-romantic work is accustomed to intensive work on parts (inevitably, since unravelling complexity and digging out unconscious meanings involve several readings). The irony of this state of affairs is that intensive study of characteristic parts could be as illuminating for Augustan as for Romantic work—granted a change of equipment: the substitution of philosophical and general linguistics—at any rate as a starting point—for the old New 'scientific' and metaphysical interpretation.

Warburton's large-scale approach, of course, would be just as appropriate for discursive prose. But then this poetry does have some kinship to the prose of its day, and we should take more seriously than we do Arnold's contention that Pope and Dryden were classics of our prose—without accepting the implication that this is a bad thing for poets to be, or forgetting that the mere fact of putting words into verse must make a considerable difference to their effect on the reader. Applied widely, Warburton's method would probably show up a general distinction between Romantic and Augustan modes. The former are the more concerned with *states*, the latter with *relationships*. However, even if such study showed various Augustan poems to have all the structural (and other) qualities of good prose argument, it would hardly placate those who want verse to have some plus-quality. (Not an unreasonable demand. Why write, otherwise, in an artificial form?) It is the contention of this essay that the intensive study of small-scale relationships—in a word, of syntax—could remove this worry and reveal for modern critics what is central in Augustanism. To exaggerate a bit: you can prove by algebra that Augustan poetry is 'poetry'.

Perhaps this is really to exaggerate quite a lot, for not only does the algebra turn out to be merely a form of symbolization, not a mathematical technique, but also it becomes evident that syntax cannot be usefully studied in isolation by the critic. In every case such study must be merely a starting-place, not a destination; matters of arrangement are inseparable—in a creative continuum—from other elements. Nevertheless, to start from one point rather than some others may have exceedingly important results—particularly, it is contended, for the criticism of Augustan works.

As Mrs Nowottny says in her splendid book *The Language Poets Use* (1962):

> The meaning of an utterance as a whole does not reach [the reader] at all unless it reaches him already arranged into the set of relations syntax imposes on the words the utterance contains. Consequently syntax, however little it is noted by the reader, is the groundwork of the poet's art. Often it supports a poetic edifice elaborated by many other poetic means and the reader is content to believe that these other means are the cause of his pleasure, but when a passage relies chiefly on its especially compelling and artful syntax to make its effect, the reader and the critic who never expect syntax to be more than 'a harmless, necessary drudge' holding open the door while the pageantry of words sweeps through, will be at a loss to understand why the passage affects them as it does and at a loss to do critical justice to its art. (p. 10)

Crabbe provides a nice test case. He comes very late for an Augustan, lacks the expected polish, and has therefore sometimes been claimed as a Romantic. Huchon, author of the definitive work on Crabbe, knows better. Indeed, he is so convinced his subject is not a Romantic that he finds difficulty in admitting him as a poet at all—though he obviously likes his work—for Crabbe rarely uses metaphor (essential for a poetry of states) and is never elevated and ecstatic:

> Poetry which is emotion expressing itself in rhythmical language, demands a bold intellect, an enthusiastic and passionate mind. Too uniformly reasonable and calm, Crabbe becomes animated only on rare occasions and emits only transient gleams. Besides, he is hampered by the prosaic nature of his favourite subjects.... Where is the spirit of poetry to come from, which alone can breathe life into this refractory material? (R. HUCHON, *George Crabbe and His Times* [1907], p. 479)

Where indeed, on Romantic principles? But the passage implies an unconsciously stipulative and evaluative definition of 'poetry'.

In any case, it is arguable that Crabbe offers something different from M. Huchon's requirement but just as good. Whether you called it 'poetry' or not would hardly matter. However, what Crabbe's verse does offer—apart from prose virtues in the content and construction of his tales, open to large-scale study —can be properly called 'animation'; and it is as fully inherent in the use of language as anything the Romantics offer. But this animation is not an emotive glow produced by the friction of verbal connotations after the Romantic manner; it is rather an aesthetic pleasure resulting from lively patterns of syntax.

Oddly, then, it may turn out that one distinguishing characteristic of Augustan poetry is the possession of a more purely aesthetic element than is normally to be found in the succeeding Romantic work which intended to rely so much less on sense. For it seems significant that Crabbe's verse which yields little to modes of analysis suitable for Romantic or symbolist work is responsive to methods suitable for acknowledged Augustan work.

No such methods have in fact been demonstrated in detail, though Davie's *Articulate Energy* gives good general indications. To speak of a syntactical approach is not to advocate one method, but a *range* of critical methods appropriate for, say, Pope but not for, say, Keats. Of these, the 'algebraic' has more symbolic than practical importance, since syntactical devices are usually either too simple to need formal demonstration or too complicated for it, too closely bound to all those other elements of meaning—tonal, lexical, implicatory—that must lead criticism out of grammatical bounds (*A* & *B* logically implies *B* & *A*, so 'She got married and had a baby' for the symbolic logician must be the same as 'She had a baby and got married'—but not for the critic.). However, a sort of algebraic symbolization seems to be sometimes capable of demonstrating a plus-quality that comes from syntax more clearly than any verbal explanation would. In *Resentment*, from *Tales of the Hall*, Crabbe writes of a sick old man's predicament in the English weather:

> A dreadful winter came, each day severe,
> Misty when mild, and icy cold when clear.

To one whose literary sensibility has not been overstimulated by Romantic and post-romantic experiment, this couplet is likely to feel exquisitely pointed if a little formal.[2] In its context of regular rhyme, metre and alliteration, the formality will seem proper enough, however (this being one of the rewards of verse-form). What is likely to escape conscious notice is that the pointedness results from an exceedingly complicated antithesis, whose beautifully interlocking implications are only just graspable as the attention passes over this little hillock in Crabbe's apparently flat narrative. Their existence can, however, be visually demonstrated.

The key words all have two semantic aspects: they are value-words, or *evaluators*, in so far as they are pointers of good or bad for the old man, and they are *sensibles* in so far as they point to physical qualities. If we let x represent the bad, y the good; a mildness, and b clearness; then, with not-a ($-a$) and not-b ($-b$) for their opposites 'cold' and 'misty', we have a simple and adequate symbolism for analysing the antithetical patterns that give to the line 'Misty when mild/ . . . cold when clear' an animation over and above the effect of metre and statement.

Firstly, there is the pattern of mixed values:

$$(x \;\&\; y) \quad / \quad (x \;\&\; y)$$

(the weather understood as bad-with-good and again bad-with-good)

Secondly, the pattern of mixed sensibles:

$$(-b \;\&\; a) \quad / \quad (-a \;\&\; b)$$

(a different antithesis given by the perception of contrasting physical qualities: misty as the opposite of clear, cold of mild).

Thirdly, the pattern of sensibles and values:

$$(-b \;\&\; y) \quad / \quad (-a \;\&\; y)$$

Fourthly, that of values and sensibles:

$$(x \;\&\; a) \quad / \quad (x \;\&\; b)$$

The synthesized perception, taken in by the sensitive reader as an aesthetic complex, is then as follows:

[2] The following two pages of this chapter, in an abbreviated form, are included in the writer's *Romantic Conflict* (1963) published by Chatto & Windus, to whom acknowledgment is due for permission to reprint.

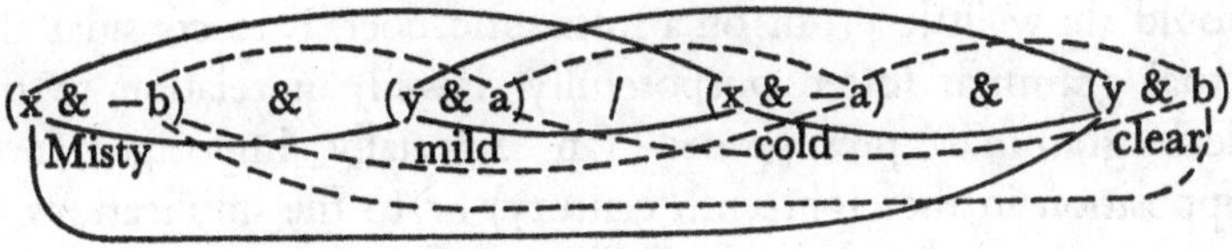

i.e. twelve antithetical relationships whose harmonies are visually demonstrable by line-linkage. The interlocking antitheses are of course alliteratively both separated (by the *m*s and *c*s) and joined (by the *w*s): m w m/c w c.[3] And the rhyme clips all this neatly to its main clause in the first line, as well as helping to make the formal pattern not unnatural.

Alliteration also has a function, perhaps rather obviously, in this couplet from *The Village:*

> Who *f*ar from *c*ivil arts and *s*ocial *f*ly
> And *s*cowl at *s*trangers with *s*uspicious eye.

But here the animation comes from syntactical variation which could more clearly be shown diagrammatically than algebraically. In the first line there is an eddy in the current of syntax. The strong impetus of the clause to get as soon as possible to its distant verb '*fly*' is swirled by the impulse to set 'and social' before 'arts' where it belongs—or where it would belong in prose. The writer is banking on the kinship of Augustan prose and verse to enable him to play off expectation against anticipation. In the couplet as a whole, too, there is a change of syntactical direction; the first verb comes at the end of the clause, the second at the beginning.

If the first variation from prose syntax has a purely aesthetic effect, like a variation in a tune, this second one serves the content. The change of structure from *subject—extension of verb—verb* to (*subject*)—*verb—extension of verb* elegantly illustrates (without vulgarly imitating) Crabbe's turning from the villagers' negative, to their positive hostility.

Another reasonably rewarding approach to Crabbe, which

[3] Even this addition of 'musical' effects to the semantic ones (of values and sensibles) already added to the basic syntactical arrangement of antitheses, does not exhaust the matter. 'Icy' certainly strengthens 'cold' thus *semantically* sharpening the antithesis with 'mild', while the long 'i' *musically* relates it to that word (so that we are less likely to miss the semantic point). Again, syntax proves to be essential, but inseparable from other effects.

would show little profit on a Romantic poet, is to consider the actual grammar (often purposefully flawed) in relation to the ideal grammar presupposed (an especially important presupposition in the eighteenth century) or to the implications of metre and word-order. The following four lines reveal several of many possible effects. In general we should note the energy obtained by using active verbs and by leaving out—without loss of clarity—the weak auxiliaries 'was' and 'were' that ought strictly speaking to be in.

1. Pinn'd, beaten, cold, pinch'd threaten'd and abus'd—
2. His efforts punish'd and his food refus'd—
3. Awake tormented—soon arous'd from sleep—
4. Struck if he wept, and yet compell'd to weep.

(*Peter Grimes*)

The most obvious effects seem to be as follows:

1. Two syllables ('pinn'd' and 'pinch'd') that are by position metrically light get syntactically a heavy stress. The effect of struggle is of course not just the result of extra stresses, but of extra stresses *against* a contrary tendency.

2. Alliteration and metre enforce the grammatical sense which is further compacted by the omission of 'were' and 'was'.

3. Off-beat parallelism and inversion. The word-order suggests a straightforward inversion, with two parts in one half of the antithesis paralleled by two in the other (a.b/b.a). But 'Awake' is not quite equivalent to 'sleep' (but to 'asleep'). The one is an adjective and indicates a time ('When he was awake'); the other is a noun indicating a state. Nor is 'tormented' quite equivalent to 'arous'd,' because it represents continuous action and is governed by a much stronger word than the weak adverbial 'soon'. Perhaps it is a rationalization to say that this underlines the idea of alternating conditions which merge into each other, but it certainly has an effect comparable to off-beat passages in otherwise regular music: it renews attention.

4. Straightforward antithetical structure emphasizing the dilemma given by the sense, but varied a little to avoid monotony (strong verb and weak; and preterite and infinitive).

But could the contemporary audience be expected to register such a variety of syntactical effects, even subconsciously? Almost certainly, yes. As a conversationalist—particularly in the Restoration period—the educated Augustan aimed at elegance and wit, and lay awake at night preparing spontaneous epigrams for the morrow. Naturally, this characteristic concern with style appeared in a higher degree in his written prose. That it should involve a play of syntax was almost inevitable. A wit depending on neat pointing would avoid any suspicion of 'enthusiasm', pointing itself suggests intelligence and therefore makes for a style aesthetically suited to matter of argument, and a play of structural permutations gives an impression of wit or intelligence even when it is not there, and keeps the attention lively, ready for when it is. At its best, as in Swift or Gibbon, it can combine the aesthetic and the utilitarian in a masterly way. Take the following passage by Swift:

> Sometimes the quarrel between two princes is to decide which of them shall dispossess a third of his dominions, where neither of them pretend to any right. Sometimes one prince quarrelleth with another for fear the other should quarrel with him. Sometimes a war is entered upon because the enemy is too strong; and sometimes because he is too weak. Sometimes our neighbours want the things which we have, or have the things which we want; and we both fight, till they take ours, or give us theirs. (*Gulliver's Travels*, Bk. IV, Chap. 5)

As a group, these sentences are notable for their difference and their similarity. Much of the Augustan dance of syntax is based on the stately counterchange of antithesis; in this case all of it is. Yet every sentence is antithetical in a different way. Thus a passage dealing systematically, and very generally, with one field of discourse offers variety in unity—and thereby combines in its texture a sense of lively intellection with a sense of strict relevance. Individually, the sentences are notable for their unexpected functional specialization. In the first, a beautifully fluid interchange—matching *two* with *third*, *which of them* with *neither of them*, *which of them* with *third*, *neither of them* with *two*—serves to enforce the theme (roughly that of the absurdity of *motives* masquerading as *reasons*). In the second sentence, the mirror-antithesis (a.b/b.a) seems to have a mainly aesthetic value. It is formally elegant in itself and it serves elegantly to contrast the next sentence whose plain antithetical structure at last puts the absurdity bluntly (a & —a). In the final sentence, now that we are accustomed to the strategy, psychological as well as logical irony is pointed up by the syntactical structure. The aesthetically pleasing mirror-antithesis of the first part forces us to see that both sides are in principle the same, logically speaking. We cannot, then, escape the biting psychological point enforced in the second part by matching '*take* ours' with '*give* theirs'.

Gibbon uses antithesis (and other syntactical manœuvres) for an even greater range of effects than Swift. But perhaps the point about reader-appreciation is sufficiently plain, without further analysis. It remains, though, to sketch—or rather to do all that exigencies of space allow: to hint at—some of the extensions of syntactical animation by a greater poet than Crabbe: the pontiff of Augustanism, Pope.

No one doubts that Pope is a master of antithesis. Indeed, it is popularly supposed that his work consists of little else. What is less appreciated—owing to his clarity—is the amazing complexity of its meshing with linguistic devices of all kinds from the sublime or the beautiful to the deliberately ridiculous. Much, then, is debarred from examination here (even if we had the space) for this essay is concerned primarily not with those uses of language which are likely to be found in any good poetry, but only with this one, syntactical, use which is as special to Augustanism as the emotional glow from a friction of verbal connotation is to Romanticism. The following fairly simple couplet from the *Essay on the Characters of Women*, however, may serve as a preliminary to other less antithetical usages. This exceptional woman

> Charms by accepting, by submitting sways,
> Yet has her humour most, when she obeys.

The second line is slightly paradoxical in its internal relationships, considerably so in its relationship to the first line. This latter relationship plays against the former, since the slight element of paradox in the idea of liking to obey would be entirely cancelled by the realization that *this* obedience is in fact a mode of rule (sway) were it not for the syntactical pull of the antithetical syntax which insists on an opposition logic could not sustain. The result, an aesthetic *frisson* comparable to that of a melodic discord. Something similar takes place in the first line alone. Grammatically, we have a straightforward mirror-antithesis (main verb. participle/participle. main verb). 'Accepting' is certainly much the same thing as 'submitting', and the structure insists that the relationship of 'charms' to the one is the same as that of 'sways' to the other and therefore that they are equivalent to each other. But neither of these things is true. To sway by submitting is paradoxical, but to charm by accepting is what one might expect; and one might well sway without charming and charm without swaying; they are by no means equivalent. Of course, 'charm' *can* mean 'influence' as well as 'please', and this secondary meaning is inevitably made present by the structure though it is contrary to the context. In terms of meaning, then, the antithesis is (a & −b): b :: b: −b. The effect of this discord, however, is in the main not aesthetic but psychological; it makes the rather underhand business of wheedling seem charming.

But more interesting than this sort of thing is the extraordinary extent to which Pope, the high priest of 'correctness', is prepared to sacrifice grammar for effect. At least as much credit must be given to this device as to the often-noted tension between colloquial language and formal structure, when we try to account for the pressure and intensity of his poetry—pressure and intensity quite different in kind from that of romantic work. It can be shown that psychological attention is not distributed evenly. As one might expect it fastens most firmly on the comparatively infrequent words that bear the burden of meaning and least firmly on the very frequent, but merely structural words ('the', 'was', 'were', 'have', 'to' and the like). This principle obviously provides the driving power behind the famous passage immediately preceding that from which the last couplet came:

See how the World its Veterans rewards:
A Youth of Frolics, an old Age of Cards;
Fair to no purpose, artful to no end,
Young without Lovers, old without a Friend;
A Fop their Passion, but their Prize a Sot;
Alive ridiculous, and dead forgot!

The terrible bite of that last line, in which every word (save *and*) hammers a nail into the coffin, comes from the omission of 'they were' and 'they are' quite as much as from the antithesis. The words left out are as much part of the poem as those put in. It is probable, too, that the feeling of climax comes not so much from the progression of the sense as from the fact that this line is syntactically more concentrated than the others (which leave out 'see' (line 2), 'they are' (3 and 4), 'was' and 'is' (5) and keep in a number of structural words).

Such grammatical economy is not exceptional but habitual in Pope, and so is much other deliberate grammatical mistaking. Mr Eliot has been much commended for a couple of daring instances of fused grammar in *The Waste Land* and Joyce for many instances in *Ulysses.* One is tempted to assert that the only reason Pope has not is that he works with an appearance of incomparable ease. The whole structure seems well cut and stylish and the stitches don't show. His is the art that conceals art. In the 'Atticus' passage of the *Epistle to Dr Arbuthnot,* for instance, we have an extraordinary sentence of eighteen lines in which the main clause 'Who but must laugh' comes at the end as a long-awaited climax, everything before it being a sequence of dependent clauses. These build up expectation, for we don't know what they depend on, since their ten completed verbs ('Bear', 'View', etc.) and five incomplete ('Willing', 'afraid', etc., which need a 'be') are all hung economically from one unrepeated auxiliary, 'Should' (which therefore fuses three operations: should exist, act so, be such—and, to begin with, also suggests the question 'Should such a man . . . [be allowed to] . . . ?'):

Should such a man, too fond to rule alone,
Bear, like the Turk, no brother near the throne,
View him with scornful, yet with jealous eyes,

And hate for arts that caus'd himself to rise;
Damn with faint praise, assent with civil leer,
And without sneering, teach the rest to sneer;
Willing to wound, and yet afraid to strike,
Just hint a fault, and hesitate dislike;
Alike reserv'd to blame, or to commend,
A tim'rous foe, and a suspicious friend;
Dreading ev'n fools, by Flatterers besieg'd,
And so obliging, that he ne'er oblig'd;
Like *Cato*, give his little Senate laws,
And sit attentive to his own applause;
While Wits and Templars ev'ry sentence raise,
And wonder with a foolish face of praise:—
Who but must laugh, if such a man there be?
Who would not weep, if ATTICUS were he?

In an interesting essay on 'One Relation of Rhyme to Reason' (*Modern Language Quarterly*, v, [1944], 323–38) W. K. Wimsatt, Jr., demonstrated the contribution rhyme may make to sense or aesthetic pleasure, or both, by setting a difference in parts of speech, or in function of the same parts of speech, against parallel structures of line or sense-units. Thus, of the four lines—parallel in structure—from 'Dreading ev'n fools . . .' to '. . . his own applause', he writes:

> Here the same parts of speech are rhymed, but one verb is passive, one active; one noun is plural, one singular. The functions are different, in each case what he does being set against what he is. (p. 332)

Most of the remainder of the Atticus passage, of course, is characterized by the rhyming of different parts of speech. Such 'irregularity' is certainly an important part of the total effect, but is hardly so essential to it as the larger grammatical irregularity. The one gives Pope's rapier its dazzling movement, but the other is the source of the killing muscular thrust.

A similar slight sacrifice of grammatical correctness for syntactical strength is to be seen in the following passage (and many others), where 'shall' must be carried on through all four lines but 'in vain' only as far as the second:

> In vain thy Reason finer webs shall draw,
> Entangle Justice in her net of Law,
> And right, too rigid, harden into wrong;
> Still for the strong too weak, the weak too strong.
> (*Essay on Man*, Epistle III)

It is noteworthy that *weak* and *strong* are each used both as nouns and adjectives, so that the antithesis of sound is counterpointed by a different antithesis of sense, and this in turn is complicated by the tonal alikeness (pejorative) in the adjectival uses of words opposite in sense. This could be elaborated symbolically, as Crabbe's couplet was. But no doubt enough has been done on these lines, and there is a risk of giving the impression that there is nothing more to Augustan poetry than syntactical ingenuity lending muscular vitality to a body of common sense—an impression obviously falsifiable (in this case by noting the suppressed metaphors behind *webs* and *Reason*, *Justice* and *net*, the ambiguity of *rigid* and *harden*, the use of alliteration, and so on).

The present approach has simply been intended to indicate the possibility of a special way into Augustanism at a point where modern criticism has faltered—a way which takes advantage of one general difference between Augustan and Romantic or symbolist works. Where they are typically concerned with states, and thus with evocative imagery, it is more concerned with relations, and therefore relies to a greater extent on patterns of syntax.

It proceeds systematically where they proceed by leaps, sparking gaps of sense, yet it proceeds no less excitingly if our attention is not misguided. Their syntax is subordinated to emotive effects or metaphysical persuasion, and if it draws attention to itself it is probably failing in those effects. Augustan syntax can afford to be so patterned as even to play a pure aesthetic of composition against other emotive effects. But it commonly subserves a general desire for reasonable, or apparently reasonable persuasion. So it comes to provide a rather unexpected sort of 'animation' over and above that of metre and matter. At times, indeed—when the syntactical form is closely linked with the matter of argument—

it provides what can only be described as an aesthetic of intellection—not the pleasure of thinking itself, but a pleasure deriving from the same area of mind: something akin to what the mathematician presumably means when he refers to the 'beauty' of an equation.

The New Critics eliminated the word '*aesthetic*' from the vocabulary of modern criticism—perhaps rightly, for it had come to be used in a vague, sloppy way. But if stylistics can bring it back refurbished, as above, that alone would justify the present attempt, for however important a work may be in other respects, if it is not aesthetic it is not art.

4

Taking a Poem to Pieces

THIS CHAPTER is designed to carry the reader of literature to the brink of linguistics.[1] In recent years a number of linguists[2] have attempted to describe linguistic features as they occur in literary texts, hoping that their descriptions might help a reader to understand and appreciate the text. I have chosen a short, recent, lyric poem. It contains no magnetic peculiarities of language; in fact most critics, I imagine, would ignore the language altogether. My hypothesis is that the grammatical and other patterns are giving meaning in a more complex and tightly packed way than we expect from our familiarity with traditional methods of describing language. Modern methods of linguistic analysis, based on more comprehensive and detailed theories of language, can at least tackle the problem of describing literature. In this paper the accent will be on grammar; there is little to say about the vocabulary of such a short text when we have no proper description of English vocabulary patterns to use as a basis; the phonology and orthography (the study of the sound- and letter-sequences and combinations) are also largely ignored—with reluctance—for reasons of space and simplicity.

[1] This chapter is a revised version of a paper delivered to the Nottingham University Linguistics Society in January 1964.

[2] For example, M. A. K. Halliday, 'The Linguistic Analysis of Literary Texts', *Proceedings of the IXth Congress of Linguists* (The Hague, 1964); A. A. Hill, 'An Analysis of *The Windhover*: An Experiment in Structural Method', *PMLA*, lxx (1955); S. R. Levin, *Linguistic Structures in Poetry* (The Hague, 1962).

FIRST SIGHT[*]

Lambs that learn to walk in snow
When their bleating clouds the air
Meet a vast unwelcome, know
Nothing but a sunless glare.
Newly stumbling to and fro
All they find, outside the fold,
Is a wretched width of cold.

As they wait beside the ewe,
Her fleeces wetly caked, there lies
Hidden round them, waiting too,
Earth's immeasurable surprise.
They could not grasp it if they knew,
What so soon will wake and grow
Utterly unlike the snow.

PHILIP LARKIN

The only phonological units which we shall need are the stanza and the line, and the first question is how congruent are the grammatical and metrical units here? This question splits down into two: what are the relative sizes of the units, and how do they fit together? Sentences are on average three and a half lines, half a stanza long. (Each line has seven syllables except lines 9 and 12, and each stanza has seven lines.) Sentences are all about the same length, either three or four lines long. There is complete congruence, then, between line, sentence and stanza, since each sentence-stop ends a line, each stanza end ends a sentence, and sentences are as nearly uniform in length as is possible. So we are given a framework of grammar and metre where there is an exceptionally good fit; there are no tag ends of sentences at the ends of stanzas, and there is no great discrepancy in the length of sentences.

Moving on to the structure of the sentences, we recognize two elements, in the primary analysis; what we call a *free* clause and what we call a *bound* clause.[3] *They could not grasp it* is a typical

* Larkin, P., *The Whitsun Weddings* (Faber & Faber, 1964), p. 21.

3 This article is not a suitable place for an exposition of the grammar which I am using. I hope the terms, supported by the examples, will be self-explanatory. Dr M. A. K. Halliday of University College, London, originated the grammatical categories which are used here. For more detailed information the reader is referred to his 'Categories of the Theory of Grammar', *Word*, xvii (1961), 241–92.

free clause, and *when their bleating clouds the air* or *newly stumbling to and fro* are bound clauses. No distinction is made at this depth of detail between clauses containing a finite or a non-finite verb, since their operation in the structure of sentences is almost identical. Using just this one distinction, we can plot the occurrence of these clauses relative to each other and relative to the lines in the poem. (See Table I, opposite.)

It will be seen that no account has been taken of two clauses in the poem; in the first line, *that learn to walk in snow* and in the sixth, *they find*. These clauses are not operating in sentence structure at all; instead they are forming part of the structure of what we are going to call *nominal groups*. If they operated directly in sentence structure then *all, outside the fold, is a wretched width of cold* would be isolated as a complete clause. There is nothing in the shape of this word-sequence to prohibit it standing as a clause, but is it not the one in the poem. Clauses which do not form discrete elements of the structure of sentences are called *rankshifted* clauses.

In everyday English, in the mass of sentences which contain α and β the sequence αβ is most common. Discontinuity, i.e. α[β] is rarer, and so is the sequence βα. The last sentence in the poem is a good example of the αβ type.

It is the only one. The other three have discontinuous α, βα sequence, and both, in that order. But we can refine the idea of discontinuity a little with reference to a particular text like this one. As we read along the lines, we can say at certain points that we confidently expect something else to finish off a structure. If at the bottom of a page one reads *He put* one expects on the next page to read about not only something to put but somewhere to put it. If one reads *He played* one is a lot less certain what will follow; in fact, if it was not contrary to normal printers' practice we would not be surprised if the next page started with a period. Now the effect which we can presume an intruding element to have will depend in any instance on the strength of the current expectations. It is clear that strong expectations have been set up in both the cases of discontinuous clauses here: *lambs that learn to walk in snow* . . . and *there lies*. . . . It is interesting, too, that

TABLE I SENTENCE STRUCTURE

α and β are elements of sentence structure expounded by free and bound clauses respectively. To account for interruptions, the symbols α— and β— in column 3 indicate that a clause is interrupted by a line-ending or another clause, and (—α) and (—β) indicate the conclusion of an interrupted clause. In column 4 is given the structure of the four sentences, with square brackets surrounding the symbol for a clause which occurs inside the one whose symbol precedes the bracket.

Exponents of 'α'	Line No.	Sentence structure/ line	Exponents of 'β'	Sentence structure
Lambs that learn to walk in snow	1	α—		
	2	β	When their bleating clouds the air	α[β]α
Meet a vast unwelcome, know	3	(—α)α—		
Nothing but a sunless glare.	4	(—α)		
	5	β	Newly stumbling to and fro	βα
All they find, outside the fold,	6	α—		
Is a wretched width of cold.	7	(—α)		
	8	β	As they wait beside the ewe,	βα[ββ]
there lies	9	βα—	Her fleeces wetly caked,	
	10	ββ	Hidden round them, waiting too,	
Earth's immeasurable surprise.	11	(—α)		
They could not grasp it	12	αβ	if they knew,	αββ
	13	β—	What so soon will wake and grow	
	14	(—β)	Utterly unlike the snow.	

both occurrences of the item *wait* are in bound clauses which either precede or interrupt free ones. Here there is a serious difficulty in terminology. A term is needed to indicate a sentence in which the onset of a predictable α is delayed or in which its progress is interrupted. Unfortunately, whatever term is coined is liable to be construed as a contextually meaningful label. I want to use the term *arrest* for this type of structure, without wishing to suggest that *any* occurrence of this structure produces an 'effect' of arrestment. Pseudo-linguistic literature is already too full of naive correlations between a noise or a structure and explicit meanings. I wish my terms to carry only as much contextual meaning as terms like *finite*, *predicate*. With this in mind, let us say that the first three sentences in the poem are *arrested*, whereas the last one is not.

In sentence 1, then (structure α[β]α), the progress of the first α is interrupted by the β. Sentence 2 (βα) by beginning with β, delays the onset of the α. Both these exponents of arrest appear in sentence 3 (βα[ββ]) where the solitary α has its onset delayed and its progress interrupted.

Next we must consider the structure of the clauses in this poem. We recognize four primary elements of clause structure, the subject (S), predicator (P), complement (C) and adjunct (A). Every part of every clause must be ascribed to one or other of these four elements (the exceptions are irrelevant to our present purpose). The subject and complement(s) are usually nominal groups, the predicator a verbal group, and adjuncts are adverbial groups. Let us plot the structure of clauses in much the same way as we did the structure of sentences. In this diagram the slanting line (/) denotes the place where an intruding clause appears and the vertical line (|) denotes where a line boundary occurs. The rankshifted clauses in both cases are part of the subject of another clause. The reader is referred to Table II, opposite.

As with the sentences, let us see how well the clauses fit the lines. Here there is a clear difference between free and bound clauses. Though simple in structure, all the free clauses except the last have a line boundary in the middle, and in the last bound one there is a line boundary.

What is the meaning of a line-boundary?[4] Clearly its meaning depends upon its relation to the surrounding grammar. If it occurs between sentences (as at the end of lines 4 and 11) it is *congruent* with the grammar, and its meaning is of reinforcement, or the like. If it occurs between clauses or at any lower rank, then

TABLE II CLAUSE STRUCTURE

Exponent	Free	Bound	Rankshifted
Lambs that learn to walk in snow/| meet a vast unwelcome	S/|PC		
that learn to walk in snow			SPA
When their bleating clouds the air		ASPC	
know | Nothing but a sunless glare.	P|C		
Newly stumbling to and fro		APA	
All they find outside the fold | Is a wretched width of cold.	SA|PC		
they find			SP
As they wait beside the ewe		ASPA	
Her fleeces wetly caked		SAP	
There lies /| Earth's immeasurable surprise.	SP/|C		
Hidden round them,		PA	
waiting too		PA	
They could not grasp it	SPC		
if they knew,		ASP	
What so soon will wake and grow | Utterly unlike the snow.		SAP|A	

its meaning is dependent on the nature of the predictions that have been set up. Thus a line boundary occurring between α and β in most cases simply reinforces, emphasizes the structural boundary. It adds, perhaps, a slight element of surprise to the occurrence of the β. On the other hand a line boundary occurring between β and α will reinforce the prediction of the β, will reinforce the *arrest* that was mentioned above.

[4] Some phonological aspects of arrest and release are treated in detail in R. G. Fowler's '"Prose Rhythm" and Metre', Chapter 5.

A line boundary within a clause will follow the same pattern, according to the amount of prediction that precedes it. Table III shows the line boundaries in this poem classified by

(*a*) Grammatical rank; sentence, clause and group.

(*b*) Type, i.e. *arresting* (when predictions have been set up)
releasing (where there are no remaining *grammatical* predictions).

TABLE III LINE BOUNDARIES (including stanza boundary)

Line ref.	Rank	Between Structures	Arrest/Release
4	Sentence	Sentence/sentence	
7	Sentence	Sentence/sentence	
11	Sentence	Sentence/sentence	
2	Clause	β/α	Arrest
5	Clause	β/α	Arrest
8	Clause	β/α	Arrest
10	Clause	β/α	Arrest
12	Clause	β/β	Release
1	Group	S/P	Arrest
3	Group	P/C	Arrest
6	Group	A/P	Arrest
9	Group	P/C	Arrest
13	Group	P/A	Release

It is clear from Tables II and III that in the first three sentences the free clauses are all arrested, whereas in the last sentence the free clause is neutral and a bound one is released. The only reason we have to expect the last line in the poem is a metrical one. Again the last sentence is quite different from the others.

One common feature of English grammar is not represented in the clause or sentence structure of this poem. This is *linkage*, words like *and*, *but*, *however*, *in fact* which occur so often in conversation and writing. In this poem, each sentence, and each free or bound clause, stands rather separate. The only examples of such words, the *but* of line 4 and *and* of line 13, link items inside clauses, and do not affect the isolation of clauses and sentences.

All the free clauses are affirmative. No interrogatives, exclamations, imperatives. Also, all free clauses are transitive, and only one bound clause is (line 2). So transitivity is here carried almost entirely by the free clauses. Fennellosa may cry ecstatically[5] but this fact in grammar is no more crucial of itself than any other. The sequence of the elements of clause structure is pretty much what would be expected in everyday English. Unusual sequences of elements of clause structure form a familiar set of devices in the language of poetry, but in this poem it must be noted that the adjuncts scarcely ever occur in other than the commonest position for them. *Newly* (line 5) and *outside the fold* (6) are slightly unusual and are discussed further below; *so soon* (line 13) is perhaps slightly in advance of its commonest position.

Two points must be made, in greater detail, in regard to the punctuation of adjuncts.

(*a*) Line 6 *outside the fold*. Note the comma preceding this adjunct. Without it one would naturally tend to regard *outside the fold* as part of the rankshifted clause and analyse as follows:

S P C

all they find outside the fold / is / a wretched width of cold.

The element *S* would be uttered with one intonation contour with its most prominent point on the last syllable, *fold*. But because of the comma, we analyse

S A P C

all they find / outside the fold / is / a wretched width of cold

and there are now two separate intonation contours, a falling one, most prominent on *find*, and a slightly rising one, most prominent on *fold*.

The difference in meaning is slight, here, between presence or absence of the comma. A point is made about the lambs actually going outside the fold. Compare the difference using the verb *see*.

all they see outside the fold, is a wretched width of cold.
all they see, outside the fold, is a wretched width of cold.

[5] See Davie, *Articulate Energy* (New York, 1958), p. 35.

Since the adjunct, in part of the surrounding non-rankshifted clause, is out of position, the total contrast is similar to the contrast between

John, outside the office, found it nice.
and
John found it nice outside the office.

(*b*) Line 13. There is no comma after *grow*, but there is a line boundary, which has something of a parallel effect, of separating one piece of language from another. Here the difference in meaning is considerable. Compare

I want him to grow like me (i.e. assuming he will grow, specifying direction)
I want him to grow, like me (i.e. specifying growth and drawing a parallel)

Because the text has an ambiguous structure at this point, the adjunct 'utterly unlike the snow' is, in my interpretation, made to do double duty. A rough paraphrase might run thus:

The snow will not grow but something else will, and when it does it will grow to look utterly unlike the snow.

These are, of course, not the only points of punctuation. For example, some readers may disagree with the analysis of lines 9–10, on the grounds that *lies hidden* is a unit which cannot be divided by a clause boundary; again the absence of a comma supports this, whereas the occurrence of a line-end suggests the division. The poet has the advantage here also of a combination of the alternative meanings.

We may now consider structure at the next rank below clause, the *group*, the unit out of which clauses are made. It may consist of one or more words, and groups have a direct relation to elements of clause structure. There are three kinds of group, as we have already noted, *nominal*, *verbal* and *adverbial* (see Table IV). Verbal groups are the simplest kind in this text, since nearly all the verbal groups are single-word, present-tense items. This is only remarkable when one thinks of the enormous variety of choices available, e.g. *might have come*, *could have been coming*, *wasn't going to come, came sailing, came to talk, oughtn't to have been going to be avoiding coming to see.* With such a restricted selection, the variations are liable to be quite striking, and as one might expect they distinguish sentence 4 from the others. None of the verbs in this sentence are 'simple present' items. Two contain *modal verbs*, i.e. *could* and *will*; one of these is negative and the

TABLE IV GROUPS

Nominal	Verbal	Adverbial
Lambs that learn to walk in snow }	learn to walk	in snow
that snow }	- - -	When
their bleating the air	clouds	
a vast unwelcome	Meet know	
Nothing but a sunless glare.		
	stumbling	Newly to and fro
All they find the fold }	find	outside the fold
they }	- - -	
a wretched width of cold }	Is	
cold }		
they the ewe	wait	As beside the ewe
Her fleeces there	caked lies	wetly
them	Hidden waiting	round them too
Earth's immeasurable surprise.		
They it they	could not grasp knew	if
What	will wake and grow	so soon
the snow		Utterly unlike the snow

other 'double-headed'—*wake and grow*. The third is a 'simple past' item in a bound clause. The only other complication in verbal groups is the *learn to walk* in line 1.

The adverbial groups are not very prominent. The three main kinds of adverbial group are the grammatical binding groups like *when, if,* the adverbs like *newly* and *so soon*, and the prepositional groups like *in snow*. In this poem the main point again is their simplicity. Of the second and third types, there is no distinction made in the poem that is not covered by facts already adduced and not worth repeating. It is useful, though, to note that free clauses are almost devoid of adjuncts. *Outside the fold*, which has already been discussed, is the only one. In contrast, and excluding *when, as* and *if*, there are eight adjuncts in bound clauses. So the free clauses have complements but not adjuncts, and the bound ones adjuncts but not complements.

The selection of *newly* deserves a note. Although an adverb, *newly* is not one that is commonly found as an exponent of A in clause structure. Its commonest place is as a verbal modifier when that verb is itself a nominal modifier; as in *a newly-advertised product, a newly-made dress.* I suppose that the average reader notes that there is something a little odd about the line, but has no difficulty, of course, in understanding it.

Before passing on to the nominal group, which has the most variety at this rank, let us note a pattern in the relation between group and line. The first line is one element of clause structure (though containing a rankshifted clause), the fourth is also, and the seventh, apart from the unstressed initial syllable. Line 11 is one group, and so is line 14. So the last line in each sentence contains but one element of clause structure: although the average length of an element is a third of a line.

Although the nominal groups are interesting, they are not nearly as complex as we are accustomed to meeting with quite frequently in normal conversation. Here is a table of them:

TABLE V NOMINAL GROUP STRUCTURE

In subject		In complement		Rankshifted	
hq	(lambs that learn to walk in snow)	dh	(the air)	h	(snow)
h	(that)	deh	(a vast unwelcome)		
dh	(their bleating)	h+deh	(nothing but a sunless glare)	dh	(the fold)
hq	(all they find)	dehq	(a wretched width of cold)	h	(cold)
h	(they)	deh	(earth's immeasurable surprise)	dh	(the ewe)
h	(they)				
dh	(her fleeces)	h	(it)	h	(earth)
				dh	(the snow)
h	(they)				
h	(they)				
h	(what)				

Symbols used in Table V

h = headword, round which the rest pivots.

d = deictic, a word like *the, a, which,* coming at the beginning of the group.

e = an adjective.

q = anything which comes after the headword (in this poem the only exponents of q are rankshifted clauses—see "subject" column—and a prepositional group—see "complement" column).

There are no numerals, and no nouns occurring pre-head (like *stone* in *stone wall*). There is never more than one adjective, and not many of those, and only in complements. Subjects are simplest; six out of the ten of them are single pronouns, and the others are the two *hq* structures and two *dh*, the exponent of *d* being a possessive deictic. Those two *dh* groups are subjects in bound clauses.

Rankshifted nominal groups are those which occur as elements in the structure of other nominal groups, or as the 'objects' of prepositions. In this poem they are again simple in structure, and regularly consist of a single lexical item, with or without a non-possessive deictic.

The complements are most complex. The single *dh* structure is complement to the only transitive bound clause, and the single *h* structure is, as one might expect, in the last sentence. This leaves us with the four complements involving adjectives, and is an interesting place to pause for a moment because these four complements also contain most of the unusual vocabulary juxtapositions to be found in the poem. *Vast unwelcome* is very unusual, so also *a wretched width of cold, width* being the odd man out. *Sunless glare* is less striking, perhaps because *sun* and *glare* are common enough together; *immeasurable surprise* is unusual particularly with *Earth's* in front. Any two of the three words might pass unnoticed, but these three in this particular grammatical arrangement look very odd indeed.

The paucity of lexical comment reflects the fact that objective description of vocabulary patterns is still impossible. It happens that our present text does not contain many strong lexical patterns; apart from those mentioned above, perhaps *bleating clouds* in line 2 is the only one that invites attention.

Parallel to the note on *newly*, above, should be a note on *unwelcome*. This word is commonly an adjective, and one of the features of an adjective is that it is incapable of being headword in a group modified by *a*, *an*. Here an unusual effect is created by the occurrence of just such a nominal group, forcing us to accept *unwelcome* as a noun.[6] The prefix perhaps regains some of the meaning it could have in Old English.

The structure of the words in this poem brings out a pattern which is worthy of tentative consideration. If we study the *affixes*, it is fairly easy to divide the *inflectional* (e.g. lamb*s*, stumbl*ing*, cloud*s*, lie*s*, fleece*s*) from the others. Of the others, there are a few that mark a different word-class from the same item without the affix, e.g. *wetly*, *newly*, *utterly*, *width*. Lastly there is a small group where the affix drastically affects the meaning of the word:

*un*welcome, sun*less*, *im*measurable, *un*like

There is a similarity about these four, so that they may be labelled *reversing affixes*, though here the classification is less rigorous than before. One way or another, these affixes reverse the meaning of the rest of the word of which they form a part. What can we say about the contribution of such word structure in poetry, and in this poem? In poetry it is possible both to have one's cake and eat it, rather more so than in other varieties of a language. But when, for example, a trade union official said recently: 'We are not yet talking about strike action', he contrived to be ominous. The paradox of a sentence like 'I will never mention the name of John Smith' has a meaning which can be used in poetry. We could describe it as bipartite: in the present case

(*a*) A statement about the speaker's future intentions. At least one possibility is cut out. By knowing something of what the speaker is *not* going to do, we also know a little about what he *is* going to do. Very little, very vaguely, but by no means negligible.

(*b*) The accomplishment of the utterance, including the men-

[6] Compare *unfamiliar* in Larkin's poem *Next Please*.

tion of John Smith's name. The physical fact of the utterance can never be ignored in literary writing.

According to the same argument, the last line of this poem contrives to begin to say something about the appearance of whatever is about to wake and grow, and it also manages to mention the snow. The importance of the latter half of the meaning is borne out by the rarity, in love poetry, of lines like:

Her smile was not in the least like the grin of a decomposing vampire

however notionally accurate they may be.

Three out of the four complex nominal groups in this poem, then, show a reversing affix. On both grammatical and lexical grounds we have shown that these places are important. The fourth,

a wretched width of cold[7]

contents itself with a word-class affix and unusual lexis and grammar.

The last line in the poem also shows this feature of reversal, and the structure of the line above it shows another device, common enough in poetry, which gives the reader only a vague meaning. It is the traditional 'brush-off' structure. 'Something I'd prefer not to talk about' 'Nothing you won't know all about in time' 'What doesn't concern you . . .'

The grammar has led us briefly into lexical and contextual matters, but only sporadically. There is still a great deal unsaid about the structure of this little poem, and even what has been said suffers by being in the nature of commentary. Grammar deals with contrasts, multiple choices from a great many systems simultaneously, and the meaning of a grammatical statement can only be fully elicited with reference to the total grammatical description. Nevertheless, the exercise shows how some aspects of the meaning of the poem can be described quite independently of evaluation.

[7] *width* is usually uncountable; the only occurrence of it with a number marker that comes to mind is *a width of cloth, this material comes in three widths, madam.*

5

'Prose Rhythm' and Metre

I

WELLEK AND WARREN (*Theory of Literature*, 3rd ed., p. 169) distinguish three dimensions of the sound-structure of poetry: performance, metrical pattern, and prose rhythm: a useful scheme as a basis for the study of metrical form as it is perceived, allowing for a statement of the complexity of relationships between levels which critics and readers may feel to exist. *Theory of Literature* hints at the relationship between the levels thus: 'the specific performance of a reciter will be irrelevant to an analysis of the prosodic situation, which consists precisely in the tension, the "counterpoint", between the metrical pattern and the prose rhythm'. Seymour Chatman, in a discussion of Robert Frost's *Mowing*, seems to make a similar point.[1] His analysis assumes 'a tension between *two* systems: the abstract metrical pattern as historical product of the English verse tradition, and the ordinary stress-pitch-juncture system of spoken English, determined as it is by requirements of meaning and emphasis'. Chatman uses the methods of one form of linguistic description—that championed by Trager and Smith—to analyse the features of stress, intonation and juncture (transition between juxtaposed linguistic units) found in eight spoken readings of the poem, and diagrammatically compares these features with 'the abstract metrical pattern' which the poem is presumed to have because

[1] 'Robert Frost's "Mowing": An Inquiry into Prosodic Structure', *Kenyon Review*, xviii (1956), 422.

it belongs to one tradition of English verse.[2] The approach of Chatman is open to at least two objections. First, it arrives at the prosody wholly by way of performance: because it does not distinguish performance from prose rhythm, the stresses of the poem are deduced from readers' interpretations, not from the linguistic form of the poem itself. We must, as Wellek and Warren do, discount certain phonological features of an individual recitation: expressive features such as drawling, irrelevant intonation patterns, variations of tempo, dialect pronunciations. This is not an exclusion of everything except the designed metrical scheme. There remains the 'prose rhythm': a composite of phonological elements which derive from the grammatical and lexical form of the poem, and which can be readily deduced without having recourse to oral renditions.

The second objection alleges the inadequacy of a purely phonetic approach for making critical statements about poetic form. Because metrical shape is derived from the grammar and diction, as well as from the metre the poet chooses to employ, a critical description of metre should identify it at least partly by reference to the rest of the form of the text. The phonological character of a poem is rarely offered as its main attraction, for we no longer delight in linguistic virtuosity for its own sake. We are disposed to consider how it works with grammar and vocabulary to contribute to 'meaning'. So metrical patterns (for example, rhymed couplets) are identified by reference to their grammatical and lexical, as well as phonological, exponents, not only because that is the best way of describing them without leaning too heavily on performance—as Chatman does—but because they must be related, in a critical description, to two larger linguistic contexts: the total metrical form (e.g. sonnet form) and the total linguistic form.

What we hear in an iambic pentameter depends on one of the

[2] This method of analysis, with or without reference to the abstract metrical pattern, has come to be one of the chief ways of applying linguistic methods to poetry. It is based on the account of English phonology found in G. L. Trager and H. L. Smith, *Outline of English Structure* (Washington, 1951). The application to metrics was first proposed by Harold Whitehall (*Kenyon Review*, 1951 and 1956) and has recently been advocated once more by Terence Hawkes, 'The Problems of Prosody', *Review of English Literature*, ii.2

mass of relations within poetic form: that between two competing phonological structures. One is the metre: a skeleton with a few regularly proportioned and articulated parts. It is built up on the basis of one unit, the foot; five feet form a line; lines may be grouped into sets ('couplets', 'stanzas', etc.) by rhyme. These three units—foot, line and stanza—are identified by phonetic characteristics. The foot has a light followed by a heavy stress; within the line, all light and heavy stresses are equated, giving only two grades of stress. The line is marked off, not only by the number of feet, stresses and syllables it contains, but by certain terminal sound-features: perhaps by a pause, but more probably by a prolongation of its last vowel and/or voiced consonant; often by a change in the pitch of the voice. The stanza is identified by its rhyme-scheme and often by a fall in the pitch of the voice at the end. Some other minor conventions govern the form of the pentameter: for example, the light and heavy stresses of the first foot may be reversed (but not too often); the stresses of the second foot may not.

This metrical skeleton has to be filled out by linguistic elements—grammatical and lexical units—which have their own expectations of phonological form: 'prose rhythm', the second of the structures I have referred to. English grammar, like English pentameter metre, has a scale of units of different 'sizes': morpheme, word, phrase, clause, sentence, in ascending order of magnitude. These units of grammar have their own stress-patterns which—and this is the whole point of this essay—may or may not correspond with those of the metrical matrix that they are made to occupy. The ends of sentences are inevitably marked by a change in the pitch of the voice; no matter how this is interpreted by different performers, it must occur in some form. Now the sentence is a unit of great variation in length, so the 'terminal juncture', as the end-marker is called, may or may not fall in the same places as the natural terminal junctures of the

(April 1962), 32–48. John Thompson, *The Founding of English Metre* (London, 1961) makes considerable use of the method. A linguistic treatment of metrics from a slightly different angle is Seymour Chatman, 'Comparing Metrical Styles', in T. A. Sebeok (ed.) *Style in Language* (MIT, 1960), pp. 149–72. See also D. Abercrombie, 'A Phonetician's View of Verse Structure', *Linguistics*, vi (June 1964) pp. 5–13.

metre: at line- and stanza-ends. The smallest unit in the metre is the metrical point: it is always ′ or ˣ ; any two in sequence are likely to be different; the order in which they combine to make up a foot is almost always ˣ′. The smallest unit in the grammar is the morpheme. It is most often a monosyllable, and may have any one of four stresses: ′, ˆ, ˋ, or ˘ in descending order of loudness.[3] The selection depends on the adjacent stresses, and these in turn are governed chiefly by the grammatical construction in which the morpheme occurs. *Greenfly* has ′ˋ; *green fly* ˆ′; *apart* ˘′; *-itab-* in *inevitable* ˋˆ. So in verse any two consecutive syllables derive their actual stresses from a compromise between two coexistent patterns of prosody: one produced by the metre, one by the requirements of the grammatical construction into which they enter, and the syllable-context in which they occur. Additionally, the boundaries between grammatical units may be adjusted to coincide or not with those between metrical units.

Clearly, we cannot say that there are two coexistent stress-systems: this would be physically impossible. We can, however, talk of two coexistent influences on the stress-pattern of a poem, or of the result on metrical stress of the imposition of the stresses produced by the grammar. How does metre found in convention-determined phonological features work with or against metre inherent in the grammatical and lexical forms chosen to fill metrical positions? I want to sketch out some answers to this question by looking at the metrical-grammatical relationship as it affects unit of two sizes: the relation between the line and the larger units of grammar; and between the foot and the smaller grammatical units.

The grammar of a poem may reinforce or subtly resist the division into lines which is implied by other features—number of syllables, end-rhyme, arrangement on the printed page. In the case of reinforcement, the lines do not have to be end-stopped in the sense that they end with the end of a *sentence*; the conditions are that each line in a sequence contains roughly the same grammatical unit and/or ends with a grammatical boundary of about the same weight:

[3] According to Trager and Smith.

As, to behold desert a begger born,
And needy nothing trimmed in jollity,
And purest faith unhappily forsworn,
And gilded honour shamefully misplac'd,
And maiden virtue rudely strumpeted,
And right perfection wrongfully disgrac'd
And strength by limping sway disabled,
And art made tongue-tied by authority,
And folly, doctor-like, attending skill,
And simple truth miscall'd simplicity,
And captive good attending captain ill—

(SHAKESPEARE, *Sonnet 66*, 2–12)

Prayer, the Church's banquet, angels' age,
  God's breath in man returning to his birth,
  The soul in paraphrase, heart in pilgrimage,
The Christian plummet, sounding heaven and earth;

Engine against the Almighty, sinner's tower,
  Reversèd thunder, Christ-side-piercing spear,
  The six-days'-world transposing in an hour,
A kind of tune, which all things hear and fear;

(HERBERT, *Prayer*, 1–8)

The waker goos; the cukkow ever unkynde;
The popynjay, ful of delicasye;
The drake, stroyere of his owene kynde;
The stork, the wrekere of avouterye;
The hote cormeraunt of glotenye;
The raven wys; the crowe with vois of care;
The throstil old; the frosty feldefare.

(CHAUCER, *Parliament of Fowls*, 358–64)

But not:

The sparwe, Venus sone; the nyghtyngale,
That clepeth forth the grene leves newe;
The swalwe, morthere of the foules smale
That maken hony of floures freshe of hewe.

(351–4)

In each of the first three examples it may be said that the two systems coalesce as far as line-division is concerned: the set of junctures marking the ends of grammatical units co-operates with those produced by the phonological units of line-measurement (stresses, rhymes and number of syllables) to produce periodicity in the distribution of line-end pauses. Pope makes his couplets self-contained, that is reinforces them as metrical units by making the strongest grammatical break, that which falls after a sentence, coincide with the strongest metrical break, that which falls after the second word of a rhymed pair. T. S. Eliot, working without rhyme, often has a high degree of correspondence between grammatical units and lines—in fact, the clause or phrase conditions line-length. In *Rhapsody in a Windy Night* we have clause-governed lines:

> The lamp sputtered,
> The lamp muttered in the dark.
> The lamp hummed:
> 'Regard the moon,
> La lune ne garde aucune rancune,
> She winks a feeble eye,
> She smiles into corners.
> She smooths the hair of the grass.
> The moon has lost her memory. . . .'

And phrase-based lines:

> Of sunless dry geraniums
> And dust in crevices,
> Smells of chestnuts in the streets,
> And female smells in shuttered rooms,
> And cigarettes in corridors
> And cocktail smells in bars.

Wellek and Warren spoke of 'counterpoint' as a product of the tension between metrical pattern and prose rhythm. Enjambment, by which a grammatical unit overflows a line-end, produces one sort of counterpoint, although not the sort that Wellek and Warren had in mind. There are degrees of enjambment, degrees of tension between the metre, wanting to make a break, and the grammar, wanting to be continuous. It seems that the smaller the grammatical unit concerned, the greater is its resistance to being stretched over a metrical boundary. Similarly, there are metrical boundaries of different weights, the pause after the second rhyme of a couplet, for example, being more 'final' than that after the first line. One might construct a scale for enjambment, ranging from cases where the greatest grammatical break (between sentences) coincides with the firmest metrical rest (end of a set of rhymed lines) to cases where the smallest grammatical juncture (between the components which make up words, morphemes) is forced to coincide with a compelling metrical break (e.g. between stanzas). Pope, who shuns enjambment, consistently makes the major juncture between couplets fit with that between sentences—although we frequently find marks other than full stop at this point. He tolerates smaller grammatical junctures at the end of the first line of a couplet.

Between the clauses of a sentence:

Some thought it mounted to the Lunar sphere,
Since all things lost on earth are treasur'd there.
(*Rape*, V, 113–14)

Between the phrases of a clause—much less frequent:

Triumphant Umbriel on a sconce's height
Clapp'd his glad wings, and sate to view the fight:
(*Rape*, V, 53–4)

This sort of grammatical run-on, with a clause overflowing a line-end, is primarily what we think of as enjambment. We have to go to other poets, more noted for enjambment, to find many examples of this, and of even more powerful forms, where phrases and even words spill over the ends of lines.

Line-end between phrases:

Here the stone images
Are raised, here they receive
The supplication of a dead man's hand
Under the twinkle of a falling star.
(ELIOT, *The Hollow Men*)

Between the words which make up a phrase: very frequent in Milton, as for example at the beginning of Book VI of *Paradise Lost*: *in Gold/Empyreal, had thought/ To have reported, the Cause/ Of Truth, my Sons/Invincible.*

Between the morphemes which make up a word: a very rare kind of enjambment because we (poets and readers) are unwilling to put a rhythmical break[4] at a point where the grammar requires a close transition between elements. Byron (*Don Juan*, XII, 75) demonstrates that, in comic verse, this trick is on a par with the other devices he employs at line-ends—feminine rhymes, rhyming two words with one, lexically ridiculous juxtapositions through rhyme:

> She cannot step as does an Arab barb,
>   Or Andalusian girl from mass returning,
> Nor wear as gracefully as Gauls her garb,
>   Nor in her eye Ausonia's glance is burning;
> Her voice, though sweet, is not so fit to warb-
>   le those *bravuras* . . .

Non-comic examples are Dylan Thomas's *the hay/Fields, the coal-/Black night*; Hopkins's *king-/dom of daylight's dauphin, all un-/warned*; Donne's *this blind-/nesse too much light breeds.*

Occasional examples of enjambment in a poem which is largely end-stopped create points of tension. So the last example I gave from Pope—for him, a bold enjambment—stands out among the end-stopped couplets which have, at the most, only a clause-boundary after the first rhyme of the pair. At a different point in the scale, Thomas's *hay/Fields* strikes us because it is the most violent enjambment in the poem. This is a matter of degree, as *Fern Hill* has a high proportion of run-on lines with a relatively powerful sort of enjambment—twenty-five out of fifty-four. Where similar degrees of enjambment recur at similar metrical positions, we have the beginnings of a sort of play between grammar and metre. Thomas, with lexical and grammatical similarity to aid him, has

> Time let me hail and climb
> Golden in the heydays of his eyes

[4] Except that between feet, on which see Part II below.

and

Time let me play and be
Golden in the mercy of his means

at similar points in the first and second stanzas of *Fern Hill*, but he does not sustain the correspondence of grammar at regular points in the other stanzas. We can hardly talk about 'counterpoint' unless there is an extensive and *regular* relation between grammatical and metrical patterns. Milton's run-on lines are so numerous that, in many extended passages, we can sense the tension between two systems, the movement of the argument (linguistically identifiable by grammatical and lexical forms) against that of the prosody:

Th'infernal Serpent; he it was, whose guile
Stird up with Envy and Revenge, deceiv'd
The Mother of Mankinde, what time his Pride
Had cast him out from Heav'n with all his Host
Of Rebel Angels, by whose aid aspiring
To set himself in Glory above his Peers,
He trusted to have equal'd the most High,
If he oppos'd; and with ambitious aim
Against the throne and Monarchy of God
Rais'd impious War in Heav'n and Battel proud
With vain attempt. Him the Almighty Power
Hurld headlong flaming from th'Ethereal Skie
With hideous ruine and combustion down
To bottomless perdition, there to dwell
In Adamantine Chains and penal Fire,
Who durst defie th'Omnipotent to Arms.

(*Paradise Lost*, I, 34–49)

But there is not the regularity of relation between grammatical and rhythmical boundaries—between grammatical caesura and line-end—which gives rise to counterpoint. We find our best examples of this in the blank verse of Shakespeare's later plays. Kermode[5] speaks of 'straddled lines', sentences or clauses which start in the middle of one line and end half-way through the next, forming a pentameter within two pentameters:

[5] *The Tempest* (Arden ed., London, 1958), p. xvii.

... Beyond a common joy! and set it down
With gold on lasting pillars: in one voyage ...
(*The Tempest*, V, i. 207–8)

Often Shakespeare makes a pattern with a series of caesurae at similar points in alternate lines:

... When he comes back; you demi-puppets that
By moonshine do the green sour ringlets make,
Whereof the ewe not bites; and you whose pastime
Is to make midnight mushrooms, that rejoice
To hear the solemn curfew; by whose aid ...
(*The Tempest*, V, i. 36–40)

Sometimes a whole series of 'metrical' lines is straddled by a series of 'grammatical' lines, offering the regularity of relation which I have mentioned:

... Whom now I keep in service. Thou best know'st
What torment I did find thee in; thy groans
Did make wolves howl, and penetrate the breasts
Of ever-angry bears: it was a torment
To lay upon the damn'd, which Sycorax
Could not again undo: it was mine Art ...
(*The Tempest*, I, ii. 286–291)

Straddled lines are very frequent in Old English poetry. They are particularly effective, because the obligatory caesura in the centre of the line invites the beginning of a clause, and yet the alliteration binding the two half-lines together resists the pull of a clause which starts with one 'b' half-line and ends with the next 'a' half-line. In the following example, the straddled lines are italicized:

Gegremod wearð se guðrinc: *he mid gare stang*
wlancne wicing, þe him þa wunde forgeaf.
Frod wæs se fyrdrinc, *he let his francan wadan*
þurh ðæs hysses hals; hand wisode
þæt he on þam færsceaðan feorh geræhte.
Ða he oþerne ofstlice sceat,
þæt seo byrne tobærst; *he wæs on breostum wund*
þurh ða hringlocan, him æt heortan stod
ætterne ord.

(*Battle of Maldon*, 138–46)

The beginning of *The Waste Land* has an interesting example of this sort of counterpoint: a series of straddled lines starting and finishing at regular points relative to the basic lines:

April is the cruellest month, breeding
Lilacs out of the dead land, mixing
Memory and desire, stirring
Dull roots with spring rain.
Winter kept us warm, covering
Earth in forgetful snow, feeding
A little life with dried tubers.

The counterpoint is reinforced by the repetition of the present participle at the ends of lines 1–3, 5, and 6: a grammatical pattern analogous to rhyme, and more powerful than the *-ing* rhyme which accompanies it. Wimsatt[6] implies that rhymes of the same part of speech may be flat. This is not such a case. Grammatical repetition takes the place of rhyme; the phonological parallelism is incidental.[7]

II

Now my treatment of counterpoint and tension so far may appear to be not at all what Chatman, or Wellek and Warren, have in mind. Tension, for them, is tension between the stresses implied by a chosen metrical pattern and the stresses produced by the 'prose rhythm' which is the grammatical-lexical exponent of the pattern. They are interested in metre as rhythm, stress-patterns *within* the line. I also have been discussing tension between prose rhythm and metre: between the phonology of grammar and the phonology which is 'written-in' by a particular metrical convention. The distinction is largely that we have been concerned with units of different sizes. My basic principle—that there can be coincidence or non-coincidence of metrical units and grammatical units and/or their boundaries—can be

[6] 'One Relation of Rhyme to Reason', *The Verbal Icon* (Lexington, Ky., 1954), pp. 153–69.

[7] Donald Davie (*Articulate Energy* [London, 1955], pp. 90–1) has a nice analysis of the opening of *Ash-Wednesday*, where grammatical parallelism is again used to link lines together.

extended to take in the relation of the metrical foot to the smaller units of grammar, and so to approach more closely the critics' view of counterpoint.

Gerard Manley Hopkins, who was outstandingly sensitive to the rhythms of English, has much to say on the subject of counterpoint rhythm.[8] He connects it with the 'reversed foot', in which the rising rhythm established in the poem is interrupted by a falling foot: 'putting the stress where, to judge by the rest of the measure, the slack should be and the slack where the stress' (Pick, p. 122). He continues:

> If however the reversal is repeated in two feet running, especially so as to include the sensitive second foot, it must be due either to great want of ear or else is a calculated effect, the superinducing or *mounting* of a new rhythm upon the old; and since the new or mounted rhythm is actually heard and at the same time the mind naturally supplies the natural or standard foregoing rhythm, for we do not forget what the rhythm is that by rights we should be hearing, two rhythms are in some manner running at once and we have something answerable to counterpoint in music, which is two or more strains of tune going on together, and this is Counterpoint Rhythm.

Chatman ('Comparing Metrical Styles') discusses this phenomenon under the heading of *metrical point displacement.* Among the examples he gives is Pope's *Thús much I've said, I trust, without offence*[9] with a reversed first foot. This is obviously a case of prose rhythm—the phonology required by the meaning—playing against metre, a metre firmly established by Pope's extremely regular couplets. Pope has allowed the prose rhythm to show through the metre at a point—the first foot—where convention permits. In Donne, who, according to Chatman, has a much higher proportion of reversed feet, the tension is less because the metrical pattern is obscured. Hopkins's 'counterpoint' is in fact high-frequency reversal; when it is excessively frequent it produces sprung rhythm.

[8] See John Pick, *A Hopkins Reader* (London, 1953), index under 'Versification'.

[9] Donne's 'Satire II' Versified, 125. The comma after *trust*, which occurs in some editions, does not affect the present point.

Sprung rhythm (which 'consists in scanning by accents or stresses alone, without any account of the number of syllables, so that a foot may be one strong syllable or it may be many light and one strong' [Pick, p. 90]), like reversed feet, approximates to the prose rhythm of English by accommodating the tendency of the language to isochronism—relatively regular spacing of strong stresses, regardless of the number of intervening light stresses—and to the occasional juxtaposition of strong stresses. As Hopkins says, occasional reversed feet set up a counterpoint of the prose rhythm against the metre, but thoroughgoing sprung rhythm is an autonomous rhythm with no counterpoint.

At this point we may recapitulate on the link of theory between the two parts of this chapter, and suggest a shift in terminology. Throughout, I am concerned with the 'fit' of grammatical and metrical units, and its consequences for the actual, perceived phonology of a poem. In a sense, the effects described in Part I are a 'large-scale' variety of those to be dealt with below: the difference is one of size (e.g. sentence/line as opposed to word/foot). Above, I spoke of 'points of tension' created by occasional vigorous enjambment or caesura-placing; periodicity of enjambment and caesura-placing, on the other hand, produces an effect which can justly be called counterpoint. The verse-form is more subtle than one totally reinforced by grammar, and subtle in a way which justifies the musical analogy: two phrases appear to play at the same time without conflict, and as in Bach they have different starting-points along the time-scale. An isolated reversed foot is analogous to a 'point of tension'; there can be total reinforcement in 'small-scale' grammetrics,[10] and there can be a situation (Hopkins's 'counterpoint') where the prose rhythm makes itself felt as something playing against the ostensible metre. But extreme lack of fit of words with feet results in the total assertion of prose rhythm.

Our observations about large- and small-scale grammetrics tend to be parallel; but the effects we describe are, phonologically, in different categories. Counterpoint and reinforcement as

[10] For the term 'grammetrics' see P. J. Wexler, 'On the Grammetrics of the Classical Alexandrine', *Cahiers de Lexicologie*, iv (1964), pp. 61–72.

described in Part I of this chapter are effects produced by the distribution relative to each other of the *terminal junctures* of grammatical and metrical units; Hopkins's 'counterpoint', Chatman's 'tension' and the processes described in the rest of this chapter involve juncture only indirectly, the feature of primary importance being *stress-modification.* I want to underline this distinction by utilizing a second musical term, 'syncopation'. Although 'counterpoint'—melodic interplay—suits regular periodic enjambment well, it is less appropriate to the effect Hopkins describes under that name, which is properly a matter of accent. In music, disturbance of an established beat by the imposition of a different, or more usually 'unsynchronized' rhythm constitutes syncopation. It is disturbance of the metrical beat by prose rhythm that we shall consider in the remainder of this chapter.

A type of syncopation may be proposed which, unlike that described by Hopkins, involves no displacement of strong stresses, and which can be accounted for as an accentual effect produced by the overrun of metrical boundaries by grammatical units. It is an almost constant feature of superficially regular English pentameters. Compare the following lines:

(1) But if for me ye fight, or me will serve
(2) Both slow and swift alike do serve my tourne
(3) But when he saw her toy, and gibe, and geare
(4) Doe love, where love does give his sweete alarmes
(*Faerie Queene*, II, vi. 34.1; 10.6; 21.7; 34.7)

with these:

(5) More swift than swallow sheres the liquid skie
(6) And all the way the wanton damsell found
(7) Tho up he started, stird with shame extreme
(8) Accompanyde with Phaedria the faire
(II, vi. 5.2; 6.1; 27.7; 28.2)

In (1)–(4) Spenser's iambs are filled by grammatical units whose natural stress-patterns correspond closely with those of the metre: rising, two-syllable. A number of English constructions fit the iambic pattern: for example, prepositional phrases (*for me*); monosyllabic subject plus monosyllabic verb (*ye fight*); auxiliary plus verb (*does give*); certain two-syllable words (*alarmes*). Lines which utilize these grammatical patterns exclusively have their iambic metrical patterns reinforced: there is coalescence of the prose rhythm and the metre. They are used either to establish the metre against which the prose rhythm is later to play to produce syncopation (so Spenser often puts them at the beginnings of stanzas) or for special effects: *I burne, I burne, I burne, then loud he cryde*. With this sort of metre, the only variation possible is in the types of grammatical boundary which coincide with the limits of feet. Although in both cases there is coincidence of metrical and grammatical boundaries, there is a difference between *for me/ ye fight* and *ye fight,/ or me* because a clause is split in the first, a sentence in the second.

But verse which is continuously symmetrical in this way is rare. It is difficult to write this sort of verse, for it requires avoidance of polysyllables, and frequent inversions of word-order (as in *loud he cryde*, which gets round the necessity for an unnatural stress on *he*). Moreover, it is dull. Syncopation avoids dullness, and can be managed without displacement of stresses. The beginnings of syncopation can be detected in (3), where the construction *he saw her* overruns the iamb *hĕ sáw*. If we have *hĕr tóy* after a juncture following *saw*, we misinterpret the grammar,[11] so we make a 'pause' after *her*—within an iamb. The perceived pause will be, phonetically, not a moment of silence, but a product of the stress-relations: the metrically weak *hĕr* is 'promoted' to a grade higher than the iambic pattern requires, though still lower than *sáw* and *tóy*. Perhaps, *sáw hèr tóy* instead of *sáw hĕr tóy*; cf. (1) *íf fòr mé*. Examples (5)–(8) exhibit forms of syncopation which are dependent on this adjustment of stress through non-coincidence of grammatical and metrical boundaries. One sort of diagramming which might be used to demonstrate this would use / for grammatical and | for metrical junctures. So in non-syncopated, or 'symmetrical' verse / and | would always fall together. But in (6) we have:

And/all|the way/|the wan|ton dam|sell/found

[11] Making *her toy* a noun phrase.

and in (8)

Accom|panyde/| with Phaed|ria | the faire.

But this means of indicating syncopation visually would need to be made more precise: / is of several kinds, and differentiation is necessary to distinguish between the interruption of a foot by / as in *-ed,/ stird*, (7), and by / as in *-ow/ sheres*, (5).

A better way will be to acknowledge the actual phonetic nature of syncopated rhythm: the iambic foot is modified by the grammar, not through the displacement of stress, but through the 'promotion' of some light and 'reduction' of some heavy stresses—the two-stress system of symmetrical verse is turned into a stress-system with more, and more delicate, contrasts. Non-syncopated rhythms need be described in terms of only two degrees of stress, heavy and light (or stressed and unstressed); the description of syncopated rhythm needs finer discrimination of stress-levels, as that of colloquial English does. The famous Trager-Smith analysis of English postulates four (relative, not absolute) levels of stress. There may be more or less in poetry. In non-syncopated rhythm there are only two. Syncopation has more than two, and, as the four-stress approach is well documented, we could adopt this and look for four. Let us apply it to some of the Spenser examples.

(8) is the most interesting. We should have no doubt about giving the highest degree of stress (4, or ′) to syllables, 2, 6, and 10—even syllables, so there is no displacement of stress. Because English polysyllabic words can have only one ′, the fourth and eighth syllables are reduced to ^ (3). The 'stresses' of the line are thus ′ ^ ′ ^ ′ : this against the background of ′ ′ ′ ′ ′ in the two-grade scheme of the underlying iambic line. The 'unstressed' syllables of the pentameter are variously filled by the lowest grades, ` (2) and ˘ (1): ` ′ ˘ ^ ` ′ ˘ ^ ` ′. We acknowledge the prose rhythm of this sort of line by saying that it has three (or four, most usually) stresses; we acknowledge the syncopation by saying that it is *a pentameter with three stresses*. Line (6) is a different case. None of the main stresses is reduced, the five even syllables all taking ′. The syncopation, in which the grammar resists the insertion of the metrical junctures *wan|ton dam|sell*, manifests

itself in the promotion of the weak metrical stresses on *-ton* and *-sell*, perhaps to ` . The same happens to the metrically weak syllables 5 and 9 in line (5). (7) where the grammar requires a caesura within the third foot, fulfils this requirement by a greater promotion: the metrically weak fifth syllable is raised to ^.

In this promotion and reduction of stresses, a result of running grammatical and metrical units gently against each other, lies the key to Pope's achievement of variety within a strict measure. Even the most orthodox-looking line may have one point which prevents our reading it with the simple two-stress rhythm:

> Say first, of God above, or Man below
>
> (*Essay on Man*, I, 17)

All is 'regular' except the first foot. Even this could be transcribed as ×′, a conventional iamb: there is not the clear reversal of *Thus much*. But we cannot have the verb *say* so completely overweighted by the adverb *first* which modifies it: the stress-component of × cannot be Trager and Smith's ˘; it must be `. Once we acknowledge this (and the grammar makes us do this automatically) our view of the whole line is changed: the possibility is opened up of a rhythm more subtle than that of the two-grade, up-and-down iambic. Pope goes on:

> (18) What can we reason, but from what we know?
> (19) Of Man, what see we but his station here,
> (20) From which to reason, or to which refer?
> (21) Thro' worlds unnumber'd tho' the God be known,
> (22) 'Tis ours to trace him only in our own.

Line (18) is much more seriously disturbed. It begins with a reversed foot which throws us straight into the second foot, because a strong grammatical juncture is unthinkable between *can* and *we*. At the ostensible end of the second foot there can be no break: *réa*| *sŏ̽n* is nonsense, so × must be promoted from ˘ to `. *But*, coming after a pause and being grammatically of little significance, is reduced to almost `, and the metrical break between *but* and *from* disappears. In (19) the clause *what see we* sits uneasily on one and a half iambs: ×′| × ; *we* is promoted to `, and *but*, as in (18), reduced. The second syllable of *station* is promoted, unlike *we* in the corresponding position in (18). The middles of (20) and (21) are treated as in (18) and (19): syllable 5 is promoted, 6 reduced. So there is some repetition of the patterns of syncopation over four lines ((18)–(21)): the centres parallel one another in the way grammar overrides metre, while the iambs which open and end the lines are treated in a variety of ways. Line (22), closing this section of the argument, breaks the pattern, offering a milder form of syncopation. The grammar resists the insertion of a metrical boundary between *trace* and *him*, promoting *him* from ˣ to ˋ; similarly, *ón| lỳ̆ ín* becomes *ónlỳ în.*

This sort of syncopation, truly a tension between prose rhythm and metrical system, is normal among English poets, and its range of varieties is exploited for metrical excellence. There is, it appears, a fundamental incompatibility between rising-rhythm, syllable-counted metres and the prose rhythms—the phonology of grammar—of English. This, paradoxically, may help to explain why the iambic measure is felt to be suited to English: not because its pattern corresponds to the prose rhythms of the language, for it does not; but because it necessitates a constant syncopation of prose rhythm against its own rhythm, inviting poets to be metrically complex, not to jog along with simple regularity.[12]

[12] Since writing this chapter I have read W. K. Wimsatt, Jnr., and M. C. Beardsley, 'The concept of Meter: an Exercise in Abstraction,' *PMLA* lxxiv (1959) pp. 585–98; the similarity to my own views will be obvious. Recently published is a full study, S. Chatman, *A Theory of Meter* (The Hague, 1965), which I discuss in a review-article 'Structural Metrics' to appear in *Linguistics*.

6

Distich and Sentence in Corneille and Racine

IN CONTRIBUTING a chapter to a collection such as this, one is necessarily lending support to two implications: that the various authors believe they have something in common, and that, whatever this is, it is in some sense novel. This much common ground is necessary, and also sufficient: a contributor might fairly think himself hard done by if he were first required to be absolutely explicit about the nature and theoretical status of his and his colleagues' attitudes and procedures and their relation to tradition. It is indeed possible to insist too soon on maximum epistemological clarity and expositional rigour; and in any case the reader may be grateful at being left to judge the individual chapters on their empirical merits, unobscured by manifesto rhetoric. Yet without some attempt at generalization there is likely to be a fundamental uncertainty of tone, a doubt—and not only in the reader's mind—about how much is being claimed. In what sense, in a word, can procedures be called novel which so evidently resemble their precedents?

A conciliatory approach to this perennial problem would prefer to define the differences against a background of the resemblances rather than the other way round. It would begin by attaching the putative novelty firmly to its parent stem, losing the difference of linguistic technicalities in the unity of respectable critical practice everywhere. One might take generosity to the point of conceding that the word 'linguist' could without serious disadvantage be taken throughout in as untechnical a sense as possible, as no more than fashionable shorthand for: a language-minded puzzle-addict; a pattern-hunter; and ultimately 'a Reader: one who looks through his text with one eye and at it with the other'. In some such way the separateness of linguist and critic could be reassuringly understated, and the way prepared for the names themselves to fall into obsolescence; for their techniques, in this metaphor, achieve more than a convergence, a total symbiosis of the What and the How. Both focus on objectives that the identity of their raw material naturally enough allows us to express in the same usefully ambiguous terms: the characterization of texts, the improvement of discrimination, the capture of one's intuitions of patterning; with at most a shade of difference (hardly more than a terminological nuance) in their preferential procedures—the critical ideal aiming at articulateness where the linguistic ideal aims at formalization.

Yet such a complete resolution of all differences demonstrates too much: if it should turn out that linguists and critics were at all like radio and optical astronomers, looking at the same sky but seeing each his own stars, that would be a state of affairs one might after all learn to put up with for a time; and in any case peace at this price, of complete loss of identity, will seem too dear to both sides. For his part the critic will insist on recognition of his special skill in manipulating judgments not amenable to methodical demonstration but for that very reason inexhaustibly challenging: there is no danger that criticism will ever run out of matter. Whether that danger exists for linguistics is not of course an immediate issue; but the theoretical uncertainty, however remote, is enough to account for imperfect communication. The linguist may show that much more of language is formalizable than impressionistic critics might credit, and that admiration of idiosyncrasy is not (to say the least) incompatible with closer definition of it; but if this is interpreted as no more than a claim to specialized knowledge of the latest instruments of analysis, and of profitable fields for them, then his contribution can hardly be more than a matter of routine technology, condemned in any case to inherent over-simplification. Much more than this is implied by any pretension to novelty of a non-occasional kind.

Somehow the linguist must find a way of separating rigour from its implications of triviality, and of accommodating continuous creativity to his procedures as to his material. In this perspective every investigation must also be an assay of the instruments it uses, stressing less their efficiency than their modes of adaptation; and the field most appropriate to such investigations will be that of literature, where the dilemma of accommodating new things to old language is at its most acute.

As an illustration of these considerations the alexandrine of French classical tragedy is in many ways particularly convenient. It is in the first place written in a highly and perhaps uniquely restricted language. With the publication over the last ten years of exhaustive word-indexes of a representative number of plays, the limitation of the lexical stock is known with some precision: 1593 different 'words' in *Cinna*, for example. This highly convenient simplification on the lexical plane is at least equalled by the restrictions on the nature, length and position of the permissible syntactic units. In such a language there will always be further rules, or further consequences of rules, waiting to be discovered; but early theoreticians knew enough of them to set out a detailed codification, and one which seems to have grown more authoritarian through the genre's long decline. Most of this codification was in fact found acceptable even by later partisans of reform. The points at issue being few and (to an outside observer) minor, and the argument on both sides concentrating on hunting out examples of non-standard lines, whether as anti-models or precedents, they provide between them useful documentation of the slightest departures from orthodoxy as then understood. The positive result, in all but the most skilled hands, was a uniformity which before the end of the eighteenth century was being likened by the unsympathetic[1] to the Chinese water-torture; a random example[2] may illustrate why:

> On m'a laissé du moins, dans ce funeste asile,
> Un destin sans opprobre, un malheur plus tranquille.

[1] See D. Mornet, *L' Alexandrin français dans la deuxième moitié du xviiie siècle* (Toulouse, 1907), p. 18.

[2] Voltaire, *Oreste* (1750) I, i.

Mes mains peuvent d'un père honorer le tombeau,
Loin de ses ennemis, et loin de son bourreau:
Dans ce séjour de sang, dans ce désert si triste,
Je pleure en liberté, je hais en paix Egisthe.

This combination of circumstances is one that lends itself well to our triple objective: to hunt rules, and through them exceptions, and through *them* rules for breaking rules; that is, to characterize the genre as a whole, seeking to express with improved consistency, or concision, or coverage, those formal rules which are common to all or most practitioners; complementarily, to isolate the exceptions to the more powerful of those formal rules and to test their correlation with literary effect; and thirdly to look more closely at the procedures of innovation themselves for any light they may throw on the central but elusive notion of the renewability of literary effect.

With a programme as ambitious as this we will be glad enough to use the hints excellently formulated by the codifiers of the metre some time before the word 'linguistics' was invented. These guardians of the law were fully aware that between the embarrassingly over-permissive syllabic definition of the metre on the one hand and matters of taste or ear on the other there is room for further tightly binding rules of a third kind; and in the substantial section of their code devoted to maintaining congruence between syntactic and metrical units they give a detailed enumeration, *in grammatical terms*, of the micro-structures that are or are not acceptable astride a hemistich-boundary:

> La Cesure ne doit jamais tomber entre la préposition, & le nom qui s'y raporte, ni entre les verbes *Auxiliaires*, & les participes que y sont attachez. . . . On ne doit point placer de suite en différens Hemistiches le *Substantif, & le Génitif*, qui en est régi. . . . Ni le Substantif & son Adjectif. . . . Ni enfin le Verbe & le Cas qu'il régit. . . . C'est aussi contre l'exactitude de separer d'Hemistiche deux Adjectifs qui se raportent à un même Substantif, à moins que le dernier Attribut ne fasse tout seul la moitié du Vers.[3]

From suggestions as specific as these very little generalization is needed to arrive at the postulate that, for syllabic verse, 'all

[3] Le P. Mourgues, *Traité de la poësie françoise* (Paris, 1724), pp. 181–3.

metrical units are ideally to be defined in terms both of numerical and syntactical components'. An earlier article[4] attempted to resume this postulate in the sandwich-word *grammetrics*, on the hypothesis that it would prove more economical to analyse metre and grammar simultaneously than separately. Certainly the postulate cannot hope for a more favourable test than that provided by the classical alexandrine, where the coextensiveness of units like Sentence, Predicate, Clause, etc., with units like Distich, Line and Hemistich irresistibly suggests the advantages of a hybrid categorization, e.g. into Distich-Sentences, Line-Sentences beginning with a Hemistich-Subject, Tetrastichs-comprising-one-main-and-one-subordinate-Distich—or such other units (the examples are intended only to indicate the kind of flexibility that might be required) as the material suggests.

Parenthetically to this last point: as long as no smaller metrical unit than the hemistich is recognized, the procedure is clearly more appropriate to the larger syntactical units. It may seem at first sight that the advantages of such wide-mesh analysis would be outweighed by the notorious difficulty of defining, e.g. the sentence. In fact, this uncertainty may be turned to advantage, since it gives a taste of freedom to choose those definitions of our fundamental units which will do most to improve the productivity of the rules we seek to formulate. What might be meant by 'improving the productivity of the rules', and other thorny issues of classification-heuristics, are not matters appropriately discussed at length here; but (to indicate one direction in which this principle may be extended), there seems to be no reason why we should not, and every reason why we should, seek *more* freedom in the definition of our units than the accident of previous usage offers. Thus if 'sentence-juncture' were defined (not without residual ambiguity) by the occurrence not only of strong punctuation but also of line-initial co-ordinating conjunctions[5]

[4] P. J. Wexler, 'On the Grammetrics of the Classical Alexandrine', *Cahiers de Lexicologie*, IV (1964), 61–72.

[5] It may not be necessary to justify this in detail, but the argument would make use of examples like lines 1373–6 from Corneille's *Sophonisbe:*

Mais quand à cette ardeur un monarque défère,
Il s'en fait un plaisir et non pas une affaire;

this would give a much greater number of exemplifications of any rule about the coextensiveness of line and 'sentences'; the number of exceptions to this and other rules might also be greater, but trivially. This I take to be one way of improving (perhaps quantifiably) the productivity of a set of rules. If there is any disagreement with any part of the procedure, it can surely only be directed at the retention of the conventional term. In any given case the decision may be open to argument; but not, I suggest, the principle. By rights, of course, the names of all categories should be printed with typographical danger-signals: in 'Sentence', or 'Clause', the term would give some sort of guarantee that the meaning was at least initially roughly conventional, while the quotation marks would claim freedom from final commitment to *any* definition (as to any rule)—freedom, that is, for such mutual adjustment of provisional rules and definitions as will improve elegance, within a given corpus.

The relevance of this brief taxonomic excursus may be shown by closer examination of the grammar of the metric-sentence. There is clearly a probability-rule waiting to be formulated about the congruence of the sentence and the metric unit, though it is not at first sight obvious which is to be most illuminatingly defined in terms of the other;[6] that is, whether a better first approximation will be given by 'Sentence-ends fall at metric junctures (i.e. at feet 6, 12, 18 or 24)' or by 'Distich-junctures are

[6] As always, this formulation is necessarily a choice from a spectrum of near equivalences, such as:

(*a*) 'At least every alternate sentence-juncture is a distich- or speech-juncture.'

(*b*) 'Non-distich speech-junctures occur only between successive distich-and-sentence-junctures.'

(*c*) 'Every sentence is either (1) a polydistich (i.e. one or more distichs), or (2) one of a pair coextensive with a polydistich, one of them a hemistich or line, or (3) one of a set, coextensive with a distich, consisting of subsets of which at least one is coextensive with a hemistich or line.'

With relatively minor modifications, this last version could also form the basis of a rule about *clauses*.

Il repousse l'amour comme un lâche attentat,
Dès qu'il veut prévaloir sur la raison d'État;

The passage is re-used in his *Tite et Bérénice*, lines 1435–9, with minor changes including '... affaire, Et regarde l'amour ...'.

sentence-junctures'. The procedure would be similar in both cases, but let us suppose that we start from the latter rule. It would then be possible to home direct on the minority of exceptions, and seek an immediate correlation between this formal irregularity and some rhetorical exploitation. But such a technique would rest on the crude fact of exceptionality; no such standardized reaction can be an adequate model for the linguistico-critical symbiosis adumbrated above. Not the first-order fact alone but the nature of the exceptionality demands scrutiny before the final appeal to critical relevance; and this shows, for example in *Le Cid*, a sub-group of apparent exceptions like lines 1145–7 or 1777–9:

> * Prenez bien plutôt part à la commune joie,
> Et goûtez le bonheur que le ciel vous envoie,
> Madame:
>
> Je ne viens point ici demander ma conquête:
> Je viens tout de nouveau vous apporter ma tête,
> Madame;

It is clear that, on a strict interpretation of our chosen terms, these examples must be judged irregular; but it may be equally clear that they are hard cases, in a sense *more like* other exemplifications than the rest of the exceptions to the rule about distich-ends being also sentence-ends. This leaves us with a choice between (1) recording a class of quasi-exceptions, embracing such sentence-peripherals as Vocatives, which affect the length of a sentence but hardly its essential structure, or (2) modifying the definition—but not necessarily the name—of 'sentence', so as to enable us to include these two as legitimate examples of congruence between syntax and metrics, and thereby to compute more accurately the rarity of the 'true' exceptions and consequently to evaluate their impact more reliably. The necessity for using the term '*quasi*-exception' under the first alternative may suggest that the two procedures are not exactly equivalent in illuminating power; but the essential point is that the choice is entirely open: those who admit to a tendency to give automatic preference to the first alternative cannot then pretend that they are *unwillingly* victims of their own categories. The example, once again, is not so much crucial in itself as illustrative of the continuous fractional distillation by which exceptionality will pass piecemeal into regularity, given sufficient and well-matched flexibility in both rules and categories. It also illustrates the kind of facing-both-ways manœuvre—rather like rationalization in everyday life—which enables impossibly severe demands to be at once met and evaded, by the discovery of a form of innovation which yet can be said to observe the ambiguous letter of the law.

One further convergent point can be illustrated by the same two examples. The first, as it happens, is the opening of a speech (I use the asterisk as a symbol for speech-juncture, doubled for scene-juncture and tripled for act-juncture); and a high proportion[7] of all vocative *rejets* are also speech-initial, e.g. the three in *Horace* (lines 515, 928 and 1065):

> ** Avez-vous su l'état qu'on fait de Curiace,
> Ma sœur?*

> ** Je viens vous apporter de fâcheuses nouvelles,
> Mes filles;

> * Le jugement de Rome est peu pour mon regard,
> Camille;

and similarly all nine examples in *Sertorius*, two of the four in *Andromède*, etc.[8] This observation suggests a probability rule under which the second example from *Le Cid* would fall among the minority of exceptions. However, the distich in question is the first, not in a speech but in a *paragraph* (as shown here by the indentation, and sometimes by a stage-direction), and so too are a high proportion among that minority—for example, both the remaining vocative *rejets* in *Andromède*.[9] It follows that we may

[7] Higher, that is, than would be accounted for by the fact that vocatives are naturally more frequent in the first sentence of a speech.

[8] *Sertorius*, *1002, *1387, *1391, *1403, *1445, *1579, *1658, *1820, **1870; *Andromède*, *769, *951; etc. Cf., for Racine, *Britannicus*, *237, *428, *461, *634, *638, **758, *779, **873, *880, **896, **929, **1027, *1311, *1387, *1402, *1614, **1617, and, at a paragraph, 1572; counter-examples at 137, 982, 1631.

[9] *Andromède*, 871, 885. Cf. *Rodogune*, 1473, 1719, 1764, etc.

be driven to stretch the definition even of so apparently unambiguous a unit as the 'speech', now to be characterized by one of *two* typographical devices, character's name *or* paragraphing; for this improves the productivity of the rule that such *rejets* are 'speech'-initial, apparently without equivalent loss elsewhere.[10] And here too the change, though extra-conventional, does not indisputably demand a change of nomenclature. After all, nothing very counter-intuitive is being said; only a (possibly enlightening) confirmation of an observation that the ordinary reader might have made without benefit of technicalities or statistics, namely that the change of subject-matter by paragraphing is comparable to that marked by a change of speaker, and might be expected to use some of the same presentatory devices. At all events, a new unit is here asking to be recognized, whether or not the name of the old one is available and acceptable.

It is important to notice that the translation into common-reader terms provides more than a merely incidental reassurance: it alone begins to give meaning and connexion to what would otherwise be merely odd; it alone makes possible the transition from 'formal irregularity' to 'correlation with literary effect'; it alone, most crucially, can stimulate the generation of more powerful hypotheses and, consequently, the renewal of the whole cycle. In the present case it is a small step up to the hypothesis that such dislocations of 'grammetrical' boundaries as we have been discussing may *as a group* be associated with changes of subject-matter generally, that is, with *cues* in the widest sense. With our attention thus specifically directed we may be led to find confirmation of various kinds and in the first place to redefine one of our categories a little more inclusively, so as to take account under one head of speech- and scene-openings marked by vocative overrun of the *Hemistich* as well as the Line or Distich:

** Que font nos deux amants, Cléone?* (*Médée*, 1113)
*** Je ne m'en dédis point, Seigneur; (*Pertharite*, 1125, 1660 version)

[10] It is true there may be as yet unforeseen snags in the concept of consecutive speeches by the same character; but this is already common across a scene-boundary, where 'speech' is respectably defined by repetition of the speaker's name (e.g. *Cinna*, 141, etc.)

** Ah! que dit-on de vous, Seigneur? (*Alexandre*, 607)
** Vous ne m'attendiez pas, Madame; (*Andromaque*, 1275)
*** Pallas obéira, Seigneur.* (*Britannicus*, 761)
** Les temps sont accomplis, Princesse: (*Athalie*, 165)

This return to the alternative formulation of the original rule, characterizing 'sentences' in terms of metric junctures as a group, rather than the inverse, seems to demonstrate an encouraging symmetry in the notion of 'grammetrics', where 'the grammar of the metrics' turns out to be only another way of saying 'the metrics of the grammar', being of exactly equivalent dramatic relevance.

A precedent for this triple association of grammar, metrics and theatrical mechanics may be seen in Mornet's remark that 'L'alexandrin classique . . . est coupé avant ou après l'hémistiche par *le changement d'interlocuteur.*'[11] In fact this formulation also survives considerable generalization in a number of directions. Thus in *Nicomède*[12] (a particularly stringent example) only the first or last sentences of speeches end other than line-finally; and this severe rule remains largely true even if we heighten the restriction still further to '. . . other than distich-finally'. Thus it seems legitimate to say that Prusias's speech at lines 1391–8—

* Qu'on le remène, Araspe, et redoublez sa garde.
Toi, rends grâces à Rome, et sans cesse regarde
Que, comme son pouvoir est la source du tien,
En perdant son appui tu ne seras plus rien.
  Vous, Seigneur, excusez si me trouvant en peine
De quelques déplaisirs que m'a fait voir la Reine,
Je vais l'en consoler et vous laisse avec lui.
Attale, encore un coup, rends grâce à ton appui.**

—has three obvious movement-cues, in this case changes of addressee; one is marked by paragraphing, the others by the kind of mid-distich pause associated in the play as a whole with a change of speaker. It seems, therefore, that we should welcome

[11] I.e., change of *speaker*; *L'Alexandrin français*, p. 48.

[12] This is one of the few texts available in a modern edition (by R. C. Knight) which retains the original punctuation. All other references here are perforce to the Grands Ecrivains editions.

the hint of ambiguity in the expression 'changement d'interlocuteur' (as much a cue in the sense of 'change of addressee' as in that of 'change of speaker') and accept, in the name of consistency, that this speech of Prusias's consists of four 'speeches'.

It may be worth observing that the phenomena here illustrated cannot be adequately described by a two-term classification into 'rule' and 'exception': a large and perhaps majority group among the 'exceptions' is itself rule-bound, at least within the time-limits of our chosen corpus. For this to be possible the primary rule must be a particularly well-populated and at the same time particularly stringent one, so that the number of exceptions can be reasonably large, in an absolute sense, while remaining sufficiently tiny, in proportion to the total, for their impact to be unmistakable. Indeed, it seems reasonable to suppose that if there is to be any standard exploitation of grammetrical cues it will necessarily be associated with infringements of a rule whose density is comparable to that of the rule that 'Distich-junctures are sentence-junctures'.

If this analysis is approximately true a great deal will depend on the solidity with which the primary rule is established; and this is more than merely a matter of raw statistics. It is as if a special stringency in certain qualitatively privileged sub-classes made it possible to establish a rule more economically than by sheer weight of numbers. To take the most obvious illustration, Acts consist of course of a whole number of distichs. They tend in fact to be composed of a whole number of *tetrastichs*; but this is a secondary effect of the dominance of masculine rhymes to mark Act-ends.[13] Monologues also begin (and in Corneille end too) at a distich-juncture[14] (or fall at a distich-juncture when they are not themselves in alexandrines).[15]

These tokens of the congruence of grammatical and metrical finality are confirmed by the converse rule that *interrupted* speech-

[13] This is a 100 per cent rule for Racine's first four plays, a 66 per cent rule for the rest. For Corneille the figure is nearly 90 per cent.

[14] E.g. (note the use of such monologues to mark Act-junctures; there is of course no need to specify when they mark scene-junctures): *Le Cid*, 237–60, 1001–24; *Horace*, ***711–64, 1195–1250; *Cinna*, ***1–52, 1121–92; *Polyeucte*, ***721–64; *Rodogune*, ***395–426, 843–96, 1115–30***, 1249–58, 1475–96***, ***1497–1538. With a little

junctures are predominantly *not* at distich-junctures. Certainly in Racine, where interruptions (provisionally defined by suspension-points) are particularly frequent,[16] and common at line-endings, there is a rule excluding their appearance at distich-junctures in tragedy. I can find only one unmistakable counter-example, at *Bérénice*, 86:

Arsace: Et lorsque cette reine, assurant sa conquête,
Vous attend pour témoin de cette illustre fête,
Quand l'amoureux Titus, devenant son époux,
Lui prépare un éclat qui rejaillit sur vous . . .

Antiochus: Arsace, laisse-la jouir de sa fortune,
Et quitte un entretien dont le cours m'importune.*

For the rest, there are a few examples of *self*-interruptions at distich-junctures,[17] and at *Mithridate*, 34, the suspension-points mark the reverse of an interruption, i.e. an encouragement:

* Je m'en vais t'étonner. Cette belle Monime,
Qui du Roi notre père attira tous les vœux,
Dont Pharnace, après lui, se déclare amoureux. . . .
* Hé bien, Seigneur? *Je l'aime, et ne veux plus m'en taire,

Similarly at *Athalie*, 144:

Ah! si dans sa fureur elle s'était trompée;
Si du sang de nos rois quelque goutte échappée. . . .
* Hé bien, que feriez-vous? *O jour heureux pour moi!
De quelle ardeur j'irais reconnaître mon roi!

[16] In *Alexandre* half the intra-distich speech-junctures are interruptions.
[17] *Britannicus*, 336; *Bajazet*, 194; *Mithridate*, 718; *Iphigénie*, 1456.

---

terminological ingenuity one could perhaps bring under this rule those apparent counter-examples which exceed polydistich length by the amount of a cue; thus the monologue-scene at *Cinna*, III, iii, consists of three paragraphs, of five, nine and six distichs respectively, plus the final line.

Mais voici de retour cette aimable inhumaine.**

Compare also *Cinna*, 1391–1424***.

About half the Racinian examples are similar, e.g. *La Thébaïde*, 591–614; *Alexandre*, ***957–1004; *Andromaque*, 591–604; *Britannicus*, 757–60***; *Bajazet*, 1429–50; *Mithridate*, 1117–26***; *Phèdre*, 813–24, 1451–60; but the remainder end less neatly, often in a salvo of short questions to the newcomer: *Andromaque*, ***1393–1429; *Bérénice*, ***953–61, mid-987–mid-1040, etc. *Bajazet*, 1065–mid-1096, 1209–mid-1250.

[15] E.g. *Le Cid*, 291–350***, *Polyeucte*, 1105–60, *La Thébaïde*, ***1203–34. The rule also holds for other inserts, such as letters, conventionally in other metres.

Comedy is another matter: in fact this is one of a number of rules of tragic grammetrics whose infringement constitutes, or correlates with, comic effect:

> * Il aurait plus tôt fait de dire tout vingt fois,
> Que de l'abréger une. Homme, ou qui que tu sois,
> Diable, conclus; ou bien que le ciel te confonde!
> * Je finis. *Ah! *Avant la naissance du monde....
> * Avocat, ah! passons au déluge.*
>
> (*Les Plaideurs*, 797–801)[18]

The pauses between L'Intimé's phrases are as weighty as those between other people's speeches;[19] and indeed there is a similar suggestion of Polonius-like *importunity* in Arsace, whose interrupted speech above would necessarily have gone on, not perhaps as long as L'Intimé's, but at least for another distich.

A convergent indication of the grammaticalization of the distich is given by the rule which states that when a distich so far departs from full congruence as to straddle a speech-juncture, whether interrupted or not, then *both* ends of the split distich, by a kind of compensatory affirmation, are required, with somewhat greater stringency even than normal, to be sentence-junctures. Certainly there are very few examples such as the following, where the discongruence is reinforced by the tetrastich's dispersion over six speeches and nine sentences, and the compensation even of a lightly punctuated distich-juncture is lacking:

> Sortons. Qu'attendez-vous? *Ce que j'attends, Narcisse?
> Hélas! *Expliquez-vous. *Si par ton artifice
> Je pouvais revoir.... *Qui? *J'en rougis. Mais enfin
> D'un cœur moins agité j'attendrais mon destin.*
>
> (*Britannicus*, 931–4)

The whole weight of metric precedence is overborne in crossing that distich-juncture, as in the examples from *Les Plaideurs* and

[18] Also lines 200, 270, 276, 700, 702, 752.

[19] As Racine's punctuation underlines:

> *Puis donc, qu'on nous, permet, de prendre,
> Haleine, et que l'on nous, défend, de nous, étendre,
>
> (lines 791–2, etc.)

Bérénice above; but whereas, with the interrupted speeches, the unaccustomed effort measured the force of an irresistible long-windedness, it here measures a tongue-paralysing reluctance only *in extremis* overcome (or rather outwitted: the unsayable name is not, ultimately, said).

With the congruence between distich and sentence sufficiently established and evaluated, infractions may conveniently be sub-classified into 'short-falls' and 'overruns', and we have touched on both; the former, and in particular their use as punch lines and scene-end cues, have been discussed elsewhere;[20] it remains to examine a little more closely how alexandrine sentences ever do contrive to run on for three, four or five lines. In the nature of the case, we will not expect so standardized an exploitation of these longer sentences; but for this very reason they may be better suited to the study of individual variations.

Distich-junctures in sentences which overrun them are often junctures between Enumerates, as in *Cinna*, 1488–91:

> De tous ces meurtriers te dirai-je les noms?
> Procule, Glabrion, Virginian, Rutile,
> Marcel, Plaute, Lénas, Pompone, Albin, Icile,
> *Maxime*, qu'après toi j'avais le plus aimé;

The example is less trivial than may appear: in Corneille at least the largest single category is of overruns of this kind, if we take 'enumeration' as covering other parts of speech than nouns,[21] for example, dependent infinitives,[22] as in *Le Cid*, 187–90:

> Là, dans un long tissu de belles actions,
> Il verra comme il faut *dompter* des nations,
> *Attaquer* une place, *ordonner* une armée,
> Et sur de grands exploits *bâtir* sa renommée.

[20] See note 4. On scene-end cues, Scherer shows that the shape of the seventeenth-century stage meant that characters entering were visible before they were audible, and that a transition passage of two or three preparatory lines was the normal practice (*La dramaturgie classique*, p. 270). He might have added that these lines (as also departure-cues) are habitually marked by a shortfall sentence such as 'Mais le voici.' and the like.

[21] E.g. *Cinna*, 217, 359, 375, 839, 1253, 1525; etc.

[22] E.g. *Horace*, 623, 653, 1317, 1629; etc.

or finites,[23] as in *Le Cid*, 1313–16:

> Ils *gagnent* leurs vaisseaux, ils en *coupent* les câbles,
> *Poussent* jusques aux cieux des cris épouvantables,
> *Font* retraite en tumulte, et sans considérer
> Si leurs rois avec eux peuvent se retirer.

or participles, as in *Cinna*, 653–6:

> Octave aura donc *vu* ses fureurs assouvies,
> *Pillé* jusqu'aux autels, *sacrifié* nos vies,
> *Rempli* les champs d'horreur, *comblé* Rome de morts,
> Et sera quitte après pour l'effet d'un remords!

or adjectives,[24] as in *Polyeucte*, 1215–18:

> Tout beau, Pauline: il entend vos paroles,
> Et ce n'est pas un Dieu comme vos Dieux *frivoles*,
> *Insensibles* et sourds, impuissants, mutilés,
> De bois, de marbre, ou d'or, comme vous les voulez:

or of course the repetition of a subordinating conjunction,[25] as in *Le Cid*, 1193–6:

> *Quoique* pour ce vainqueur mon amour s'intéresse,
> *Quoiqu*'un peuple l'adore et *qu*'un roi le caresse,
> *Qu*'il soit environné des plus vaillants guerriers,
> J'irai sous mes cyprès accabler ses lauriers.*

All these examples, and the many similar ones that could be quoted, show close parallelism on a number of points greater than may first appear: (i) as with split distichs, and perhaps for the same reasons, both the preceding and following distich-junctures are sentence-junctures; (ii) there may also be intermediate sentence-junctures (in positions defined by rule (*c*)(2) in note 6), but the majority are tetrastich-sentences, and in verbal enumerations these are rarely completed without the aid of a co-ordinating conjunction at the head of the sixth or seventh hemistich; (iii)

[23] E.g. *Rodogune*, 5, 261, 273, 741; etc.

[24] E.g. *Horace*, 297, 1105, 1209; etc.

[25] If the definition is extended a little further to cover the enumeration of assorted groups like *que de*, *après avoir*, etc., there are sixteen examples in *Polyeucte* alone: 67, 81, 105, 283, 511, 759, 963, 1197, 1271, 1345, 1505, 1649, 1651, 1673, 1709, 1799.

most significantly, the hinge of the overrun, that is the first[26] word of the new distich, is necessarily prefigured somewhere in the first distich (and often re-echoed later in the second) by its exact structural match.[27] In short, overrun by enumeration, like vocative *rejets*, prolongs the sentence at no cost in further complexity of its essential structure.[28] To count it as an evasion rather than an exception is the only way to give proper appreciation, once again, to the 'true' exceptions—or what will pass as such until the next distillation.

On the various other ways in which a sentence may cross a distich-juncture only the briefest preliminary report can be given here. The simplest device may be called the 'duplex quatrain', more or less visibly derived from a version half as long:

Mais cette amour si ferme	et si bien méritée
Que tu m'avais promise,	et que je t'ai portée,
Quand tu me veux quitter,	quand tu me fais mourir,
Te peut-elle arracher une larme,	un soupir?
	(*Polyeucte*, 1243–6)

These are not, for obvious reasons, common in skilled writers; but they suggest the advantages of comparing distich-junctures in tetrastich-sentences with line-junctures in distich-sentences, and perhaps also with hemistich-junctures in line-sentences.

Common in all these positions is a juncture between Main and Subordinate clause (or *vice versa*): compare, from *Horace:*

Puisque vous combattez, sa perte est assurée;
(367)

[26] Occasionally the first word in the *second* hemistich: *Le Cid*, 179, 1753; *Horace*, 105, 471; *Cinna*, 941, or, very rarely, the last, as in *Polyeucte*, 829, with inversion:

A chaque occasion de la cérémonie,
A l'envi l'un et l'autre *étalait* sa manie,
Des mystères sacrés hautement *se moquait*,
Et *traitait* de mépris les Dieux qu'on invoquait.

[27] Which can therefore act as an early signal of the long sentence.

[28] This special status of enumeration-sentences gives more solid grounds than were advanced before for allowing line-initial co-ordinating conjunctions to be sentence-markers.

Mais puisque d'un tel crime il s'est montré capable,
Qu'il triomphe en vainqueur, et périsse en coupable.
(1487–8)

Et puisque c'est chez vous que mon heur et ma flamme
M'ont fait placer ma sœur et choisir une femme,
Ce que je vais vous être et ce que je vous suis
Me font y prendre part autant que je le puis;
(359–62)

Similarly any of the metric junctures may fall between Subject and Predicate (usually buffered by some Adjunct or Qualifier). Other grammatical junctures, however, are not equally permissible at all metric junctures: thus it is not uncommon for a hemistich to begin with a participle (again usually buffered from its auxiliary):

*** Ainsi Rome n'a point   séparé son estime;
(*Horace* 347)

but rare for an even line or a distich to do so, unless in the course of an enumeration, as in the example from *Cinna* quoted above. Again, a hemistich or even line may begin with a dependent infinitive, but not, in Corneille, a distich (unless in enumeration), and this restriction is observed by Racine at first,[29] though he later takes the freedom to begin a distich with an unanticipated dependent infinitive:[30]

Ah! qu'il eût mieux valu, plus sage et plus heureux,
Et repoussant les traits d'un amour dangereux,
Ne pas laisser remplir d'ardeurs empoisonnées
Un cœur déjà glacé par le froid des années!
(*Mithridate*, 1417–20)

In the special case of distich overrun which constitutes the 'contra-distich', i.e. a sentence consisting of two non-rhyming lines, their structure in Corneille can only be of the Subordinate/Main (or occasionally of the Subject/Predicate) pattern:[31]

[29] E.g. *Alexandre*, 710 var., 717, 769, 1171, 1287, 1319; etc.

[30] Also *Bajazet*, 1008–10, 1316–18, 1733–5, 1743–5; etc.

[31] Cf., also subordinated with *puisque*, *Horace*, 628–9, 814–15, 1262–3; with *si* or *comme*, *Le Cid*, 1600–1; *Horace*, 524–5, 1004–5; *Polyeucte*, 794–5, 1096–7, 1254–5.

Et puisque vous trouvez plus de charme à la plainte,
En toute liberté goûtez un bien si doux;

(*Horace* 508–9)

—whereas in Racine's contra-distichs the line-end may also fall between Auxiliary and Infinitive:

La fureur m'emportait, et je venais peut-être
Menacer à la fois l'ingrate et son amant.

(*Andromaque*, 726–7)

Elle m'a vu toujours ardent à vous louer,
Répondre par mes soins à votre confidence.

(*Bérénice*, 1438–9)

These latter suggestions, need it be said, are still tentative, and must remain so until tested on a wider range of texts, perhaps with the assistance of a computer. Meanwhile we must hope that enough has been said to indicate, at least, in general terms, how this kind of analysis may assist discrimination.

7

'Linguistic' Reading: Two Suggestions of the Quality of Literature

IT CANNOT be taken for granted that the features which distinguish literature from non-literature are describable in linguistic terms; it is entirely possible that the many objective differences which would be revealed by a complete linguistic description of Shakespeare's Sonnets and of a theatre programme would not of themselves permit us to distinguish between the similarly complete descriptions of two other texts and say with confidence that one was literature and one was not. The problem resembles that of defining 'literature' in the abstract, as distinct from pointing to a corpus, only the fringes of which are in dispute, and saying 'that is literature'. The conclusion is that anyone proposing to describe literature in linguistic terms must be prepared to find that his quarry has escaped him, being arbitrarily defined by an unsympathetic audience as a matter of soul not made manifest in arms and legs.

This is perhaps part of the reason for a certain contemporary sparsity of descriptions of what one might have thought the most attractive objects of linguistic description, the acknowledged great users of language who have produced literature. The annotation of their texts was the first activity of philology, and it is curious that present-day linguists, claiming to go beyond mere verbal annotation to the structure and philosophy of language, should not have more to say about a level of engagement with literary texts which tries to go beyond verbal annotation. It is not, presumably, because we are convinced that to go beyond that is to enter a realm sacred to the literary critic and forbidden to us.

The approach set out here is obviously tentative and opportunist, for merely to use linguistic terms does not guarantee that what one produces will be linguistic description; it may well be rather simple literary criticism cloaked by unfamiliar jargon. For this reason it seems desirable to review briefly some other methods of approach which are methodologically purer, and explain why they have not been adopted here.

The first and most widely spread is the brisk no-nonsense procedure of describing literature as if it were an ordinary section of discourse, ignoring the fact that it is literature. The analysis of a literary text produced by this method is clearly comprehensive and efficient, and in so far as the literary values must have as exponents the structures and lexis of the passage, the method is entitled to claim that its description includes the exponents of literary values somewhere in itself, though it may not be able to put its finger on them. It is this of course which is the snag: to be able to say only 'The values are in here somewhere' does not make them easier to point to, and has not helped the criticism and comprehension of the text as literature. It may be very helpful to the comprehension of the text itself, and this essential preliminary cannot be neglected. The method becomes dangerous only when it assumes that it has, by completing a dissection and finding no soul, disproved the existence of any soul; the danger is then that it makes the linguistic approach vulnerable to criticisms like those of Browning's Prior:

> Your business is not to catch men with show,
> With homage to the perishable clay,
> But lift them over it, ignore it all,
> Make them forget there's such a thing as flesh.
> . . . Give us no more of body than shows soul.
> . . . Paint the soul, never mind the arms and legs.

A more moderate, yet still linguistic reader is able to refute the purist criticism with Fra Lippo Lippi's reply:

Now, is this sense I ask?
A fine way to paint soul by painting body
So ill, the eye can't stop there, must go further
And can't fare worse!

A second approach seems almost to make the distinction between literature and ordinary language to the disadvantage of the former. When ordinary discourse is seen to be firmly rooted in a context of situation, literature may seem devoid of the immediate relevance to an existing situation which even such a paltry daily utterance as 'Good morning' has. This concentration on the fictive, 'unreal' aspects of literary language, so unamenable to the disciplines of communication theory, is apt to lead to an ideal which is 'literary' in its worst sense. The literary language *par excellence* will be pure, abstract and distant, remote from both the language of men and particular situations. The approach does violence to what is surely the common feeling, that the language of literature is that of everyday life plus some particular fitness of agreement, not that it is a watered-down version of common speech.

The most ambitious programme is that which seeks a sort of Fermat theorem, a formula in linguistic terms which will generate literature and only literature. This involves the assumption that it is possible to prescribe in linguistic terms alone the sufficient and necessary conditions for the production of all the sentences of the literature of the past, as well as those of what will come to be recognized as having been the literature of the future. The analogy which has led to this way of thinking is the concept of the grammar which generates all the grammatical sentences of a language and none of the ungrammatical ones, or at least of grammars which generate only grammatical sentences.

The reason for looking beyond these three approaches is that they do not help the teaching of literature, do not give even a modest insight into the way literature works as literature. The first by treating a Hamlet soliloquy in the same way as the utterances of a housewife buying vegetables may unwittingly encourage the student to assume that the differences between the two can safely be ignored. The second greatly exaggerates the importance of the fictive element in literature, and stresses too highly its universality. Most readers must have felt a greater conviction that successful communication between another and themselves has taken place after reading some poems than after hearing some lectures, and it seems doubtful whether the different grades of reality to be attributed to a living neighbour's conversation, a living author's recital of his own work, a dead author's poem *in propria persona* and a dead author's dramatic monologue, are really constants which are linguistically relevant. The only case in which it seems possible to demonstrate this is that of the changed readings of Old Norse sagas brought about by a change in beliefs about their historicity and sophistication. The third approach reflects a computer age at its worst, and seems to assume that the study of language in the art of literature is the establishment of a formula of lowest common multiples, similar to that evidently used in the production of much successful entertainment, a repetition of previously successful elements to achieve an even greater success.

This is no defence of the observations on differences between literary and non-literary usage which follow, but it may be an excuse for them. Some of the differences at least are significant, not trivial, and some may be definingly characteristic.

It is as well to begin by disposing of some obvious differences that *are* trivial. In spite of etymology, the distinction between spoken and written forms of language is not relevant to literature, nor is the use of a particular vocabulary. As far as the *use* of language is concerned, the fact that literature is largely autotelic and most other uses of language are teleologically determined does not seem to make as much difference as one might think. This is presumably because in most literature the language at any rate makes a pretence of being teleologically determined: the author almost invariably has an audience of some sort in mind, with whom he desires some sort of communication. If the antithesis between autotelic/teleologically determined is not useful, is any more to be expected from that between traditional and contemporary? The poetic archaism may occur only in poetry, but not in every poem. And it has perhaps also appeared in the higher-class advertisements; the structures of Joyce and Cummings have appeared in other equally high-class advertisements.

No one at present would expect to find some infallible purely linguistic criterion for distinguishing between good and bad literature, and it is very unlikely that anyone judged on linguistic criteria alone in the past. It is important to recognize that there can be no question of the differences here called significant being so because they are decisive, and distinguish good from bad or literature from non-literature. They are significant because they relate to the creator's and the recipient's use of language; one should not think only of the author's side of the matter, for whilst it is 'his' choice of words and structures it is not only 'his' situation but his reader's also.

There are two differences between literature and non-literature which I find significant, and they are both features of our response to language, not of our composition in it. The first of these differences involves the relationship between the language and the decisive context of situation, the other the nature of the range of usage to which we refer in responding to the language, particularly the width or narrowness of the range and its homogeneity. If the relationship or reference is of a certain kind it seems to me overwhelmingly probable that the language is literature or bound to become so.

In ordinary discourse the relationship between language and context of situation whilst subtle and flexible is unambiguous enough. The language used is partly determined by the context of situation, as well as by what is to be communicated; at a funeral a curate will inform a bishop that he is standing on his toe in a way significantly different from the way the same information is passed between two dockers at a football match. The language is dependent on the situation as well as the speakers, and the situation is apparent to both parties concerned. In literature on the other hand we know nothing of the imagined situation until the author has told us; our knowledge of the situation is derived from the language. The derivation may be at one remove, as we may be influenced by the reported experience of previous readers or audiences, which was itself of course similarly derived from the language of the text. Instead of choosing our register to be appropriate to the situation, we choose (mentally, by imagining the 'scene') a situation appropriate to the register the author is using. This may then 'feed back' and affect our attitude to the register the author is using. The simplest case may be analogous to a stage direction, 'the very houses seem asleep' of Wordsworth, but some very subtle effects can be involved, so that the language is working on at least two levels, to communicate what is to be communicated *and* the circumstances under which it is being communicated without having recourse to anything as crass as a stage direction or an adverb of manner. A good example of this is the last speech of Othello, analysed by T. S. Eliot in his essay *Shakespeare and the stoicism of Seneca.*

> What Othello seems to me to be doing in making this speech is *cheering himself up*. He is endeavouring to escape reality, he has ceased to think about Desdemona, and is thinking about himself. Humility is the most difficult of all virtues to achieve; nothing dies harder than the desire to think well of oneself... He takes in the spectator, but the human motive is primarily to take in himself.[1]

It is important to remember that this is a comment on Shakespeare's text, not on one particular actor's interpretation of it. How can one set about finding warrant for it in the text? How can one tell if a character is cheering himself up? There is surely no useful sense in which one can compare Othello's speech with the speech one can imagine a contemporary making if he were cheering himself up. Examination of the 'not wisely but too well' formula may on the other hand be useful. It is easy enough to see the exculpatory tone built in to it. How severely excessive is 'too well'? Presumably one can only do something too well if it is the sort of thing in which the ideal is a wise moderation a good deal less than doing well. Is love an activity of this kind? And does Shakespeare think this? Do we think this?

It becomes apparent that because of the nature of the relationship between language and context of situation in literature, the

[1] *Selected Essays*, 3rd ed., London, 1951, pp. 130–1.

language of literature has to be highly contextually determined in a special sense. It must fit one situation only, and fit it with such a high degree of specificity that it will call forth that situation or something very like it, in the imagination of a normally competent reader. Dramatic poety has the advantage of being able to call on the services of a trained body of interpreters who because they are sensitive to these implications in the language of a text can restore all the other normal accompaniments of gesture and inflection so that audiences, less sensitive, receive a sort of reconstitution of the author's original intention. A possible gain from a good exposition of the way literature works would be to make the hearers able to be their own actors, but the point is not of course restricted to dramatic poetry.

Some of the most interesting cases are those in which what is being communicated seems to be primarily a context of situation, and not the overt content of the text. This it seems to me is often the case in Pope, and a good example is to be found in the *Epistle of the Use of Riches.*

> 'God cannot love (says Blunt, with tearless eyes)
> The wretch he starves'—and piously denies:
> But the good Bishop, with a meeker air,
> Admits, and leaves them, Providence's care.

It is surely so obvious as to be scarcely worth pointing out that this is not intended to evoke a genuine tripartite conversation between Blunt, the Bishop and Pope. The use of direct speech for Blunt's sufficiently hypocritical view thus only accentuates the even greater hypocrisy of the Bishop by the relegation of his view to a (characteristically?) indirect form of reported speech. And both views appear as cruelly realistic caricatures rather than the views themselves. The force of the 'stage directions' ('with tearless eyes', 'with a meeker air') is then to create a context of situation of easy malicious conversation between Pope and the reader. In this context 'good', 'meeker', 'Providence' are as it were devalued and made mere pronouns for themselves. 'Good' is not really the 'good' of common usage, nor is 'meeker' what a census of its occurrences would suggest. It is much more a matter of 'what passes for good, but you and I know better'. And Providence, whatever Pope himself would have said he believed if asked, is in this context practically a nullity. It may be objected that this is quite ordinary irony, but the point here is that this irony is derived from an imagined context of situation which is built into the text and not signalled by devices of intonation, supra-segmental phonemes and so on. It is this 'building-in' which seems to me characteristic of language in literature as distinguished from language in ordinary discourse. The reader is, for instance, uncertain to begin with whether the adversative 'But the good Bishop' is comparing the Bishop (to his advantage) with God or with Blunt. The sense of let-down with which the reader finds that the Bishop eventually does no more than Blunt owes much to the expectations aroused by the 'but'. It is paradoxically the inappropriate use of the small conjunction that sets the tone of accomplished confident mastery in the use of language, and this use is only appropriate in this context of situation.

This fairly simple example may serve to introduce the idea of language in literature as having a very large degree of 'building-in' to the language of elements which in non-literary language would remain outside the grammar and lexis, and be apprehended from the context of situation. I know of no better starting-point for a discussion of this question than an article by E. G. Stanley on 'Old English Poetic Diction'.[2] On p. 428 he observes:

> There is the further difficulty that it is not always possible to distinguish the living from the dead metaphor, alive only to the philologist at all times conscious of the origins. Dead metaphors can have no place in this discussion of the living mode of O.E. figurative thought. It must begin with the literalness of devices like the very common poetic circumlocution describing advancing warriors as bearing forward their arms or armour. This circumlocution is not so much the result of figurative thought as of the requirements of the metre; for the metre depends on nouns rather than verbs for stress. The lack of directness based on heavily stressed nouns gives great dignity to the advance of the warriors.

[2] 'Old English Poetic Diction and the Interpretation of *The Wanderer*, *The Seafarer* and *The Penitent's Prayer*,' *Anglia*, lxxiii (1955), pp. 413–66.

He similarly (p. 433) explains the structure of Old English poetic compounds in these terms: the second element determines the gender and takes the inflexional endings, thus determining the function of the compound in the sentence. This results in 'the substantival solidity which is a marked feature of the alliterative metre, and the direct consequence of its rules'.

But how likely is it that the structure of Old English poetic diction is caused by the requirement of its metre that nouns rather than verbs received strong metrical stress? If the account offered of its effects were adequate, one might have to accept this to be a surprising way of describing the situation, but I do not think it is. In his first example, *Beowulf*, ll. 291–2[3]

Gewitaþ forð beran
wæpen ond gewædu,

the reference to weapons and equipment does not perhaps do more than as it were 'objectify' the movement. In the second example, however, *Beowulf* ll. 333–5, it is surely clear that more than this is happening.

Hwanon ferigeað ge fætte scyldas,
græge syrcan, ond grimhelmas,
heresceafta heap?

What is the difference between saying 'Whence do you bring your plated shields, grey mailshirts, masked helmets, group of war spears?' and 'Whence did you come [*hwanon comon ge mid scyldum*] with your plated shields etc. etc. etc.?'? It may seem pretentious to assert that all syntax implies an analysis (however implicit) of experience, and dangerous to assume without an extensive survey of actual practice that the apparently natural conclusions from differing syntagmas actually coincide with differing objective states. 'Hearing the scream, I stopped the car'; 'I stopped the car as soon as I heard the scream'; 'I heard the scream, I stopped the car'; these might all be used of the same objective phenomena, but it seems natural to conclude that they

[3] These two examples are cited by Stanley from R. Heinzel, *Über den Stil der altgermanischen Poesie* (Quellen und Forschungen x), Strassburg, 1875.

reflect different analyses. A possible answer then to the question asked above is that the second version 'Whence do you come with your plated shields etc?' implies a distinction between the coming and the appearance which is absent from the first, and thus lacks the immediacy of it.

It seems to me more likely that Old English poets favoured the first because this was the way they analysed the phenomenon—and it is a way more useful to literary effect—than that they did so in order to get the requisite metrical stresses for the verse line. The question is most usefully considered as one of the indication of modifiers and their relation to the basic syntax pattern. The second version starts with the subject-verb nexus and adds on the modifiers outside this. The first builds them into the nexus itself and not by any technique of subordinating adverbial or adjectival clauses.

This has one rather odd consequence. A sort of 'free space' is created, a position in the sentence in which word substitution over a fairly wide range can take place without alteration in what one might call the prose meaning of the sentence. If 'to carry shields from A to B' equals 'to go from A to B' then so do 'To carry sword, spear or gold from A to B'. This 'free space' can then be used, and most would agree is so used, to signal minor variations in the manner of the going, so that to carry shields suggests helpful defence, swords noble aggression and spear more general aggression (often, in Old English, revenge). There is occasionally a second level present, as the helmet may be a masked helmet so that one cannot see the expression on the face beneath it, which may nevertheless be as bold as that on the face-mask of the Sutton Hoo helmet (*heard under helme* 342), or the shield may be plated with gold, so that the associated magnificence is built firmly into the actual coming in a simultaneity of awareness of both.

This absence of techniques of grammatical subordination, more common to the experience of present-day readers, is of course connected with the question of parataxis in Old English, discussed by S. O. Andrew in *Syntax and Style in Old English.* In this by an interpretation of the so-called 'principal sentences beginning with *þa'* as adverbial clauses of time he achieves a *tour de force*. One would have to be insensitive not to prefer his rendering of *Beowulf*, 461 seq. 'When the Weders for fear of attack could no longer keep him he sought thence the South Danes, when I had just begun to rule since Heregar, Healfdenes heir, a better man than me, was dead', to the received 'Then the Weders for fear of attack could not keep him. Thence he sought the South Danes. Then I had just begun to reign. Then Heregar was dead, Healfdene's son. He was better than I'.

A very obvious example of the use of 'free space' simply as time delay may serve to introduce a more interesting one.

Denum eallum wæs,
winum Scyldinga weorce on mode
to geþolianne, ðegene monegum,
oncyð eorla gehwæm, syðþan Æscheres
on þam holmclife hafelan metton.

(*Beowulf* 1417)

The order of the last clause shows clearly that the effect aimed at is one of suspense. The verb was has two complements, pain and distress, but the subject Danes is rewritten no less than four times. The four parallel exponents add little of significance; they serve merely to increase the suspense, by delaying the discovery of Æschere's severed head.

The expansion in *Beowulf* 1285 is of a very different order. 'The menace was less even by so much as the power of a woman is less than that of a man in (battle).' But 'battle' is expressed as

[Wæs se gryre læssa
efne swa micle, swa bið mægþa cræft,
wiggryre wifes be wæpnedmen,]
þonne heoru bunden, hamere geþruen,
sweord swate fah swin ofer helme
ecgum dyhtig andweard scireð.

One might imagine an amplification of 'battle' as 'battle, when the sword cleaves the helmet'. The point here is that the Old English poetic style *substitutes* this array of fragmentary immediate impressions for the word 'battle', keeps everything on the same line and resolutely refuses to analyse the phenomenon into kernel and adjectival trimmings. It is not simply a substitution of strongly stressed nouns for weaker verbs and adjectives as implied by the examples used by Stanley, but an embodiment, close-up and breathless because unsubordinated, of the impressions of battle, effective as a more sophisticated abstraction cannot be.

> When sword bound hilted hammer-forged
> sword bloodstained, helmet's boar-image
> mighty blade edges, opposing shears away

The three 'a' half-lines are re-writings of the subject, S_1 S_2 S_3 from different points of view of increasing menace. The descriptive 'hammer-forged' is not irrelevant amplification giving dignity, but an admirable example of the way in which the 'free space' made available by the style can be used to incorporate in the SVO structure a very good physical correlative for the force behind the sword-blow (just as *feola laf*, *hildegicelum* in similar situations elsewhere in the poem serve to build in immediate impressions of brittle sharpness or cold brilliance). Does the process of commutation add to the effect? The recognition successively of S_1 S_2 S_3 presumably meant less to the habitual audience than it now does to us, unaccustomed to the possibilities of a more highly inflected English, but it is interesting that one of the most 'poetic' features of Old English poetic style should lend itself so readily to this sort of structural analysis. It seems that there is at least some case for saying that the language of literature very often has a relation to context of situation interestingly different from that taken as normal, in that it succeeds in building the context of situation into itself, rather than as more usually happens being itself determined by the context of situation.

The second suggested characteristic difference between literature and non-literature concerns the field of usage scanned by the reader to establish his response to individual words. Even to begin to deal with this would require many more examples than the space of this volume permits; but a very tentative sketch may suggest a possible approach.

It is possible that the difference lies in the fields of usage from which the content of the word is derived, or in the relative importance attached to different parts of the field. In ordinary discourse the decisive reference is to the usage of living speakers of the language, the contexts in which for them a word is acceptable. The effective reference will not be to *all* contexts of *all* speakers (they are not accessible to an individual), as different groups will be given different weightings, and the individuals' background and preferences will exert a certain influence, but there will at any rate be general agreement on the central factor to which these subsequent modifications apply. This situation does not obtain so clearly when we consider the field of usage to which we refer for a word occurring in a piece of language recognized by us as literature. In this case, the decisive usage may well be that of a preceding period, and there seems to be a widespread tendency to reject with confidence many usages of many speakers as quite irrelevant to the interpretation of the text in question. Obviously one cannot make a rigid distinction; the words in commonly read literature must be acceptable in some sense to contemporary speakers, who must have some contexts in which they would accept, if not necessarily use them, otherwise the literature becomes a dead literature. At the risk of becoming involved in a circular argument one must point out that these contexts may well seem to contemporary speakers more or less literary, that is so heavily influenced by and referential to literature that they are to be grouped with literature as derivative from it and from education in literature, and not as part of the commonly available corpus of the language.

This difference of attitude will naturally be most marked when the literature involved is not contemporary, and at any time this makes up most of the literature being read. But it can also arise in contemporary literature. 'Sindark' in 'Night's sindark nave' (Joyce, *Chamber Music*) is in my experience regularly pronounced by students meeting it for the first time as ′ ˣ not ′ ′, and the relationship between the elements of the compounds gives rise to considerable discussion (dark as sin, with sin, for sin, by sin?). The reader not only seems to react as if he were more on his own, less sure of the support of the usage of his fellows, but to make an attempt consciously to seek outside the field that he is confident of as accepted usage. It is of course extremely difficult to describe precisely the reactions of other readers in this sort of situation but the above is assented to by many as a fair picture.

The situation is most recognizable in its most marked form, the response to the literature of a former age; an example is this passage on Sleep by Sir Philip Sidney.

> The baiting-place of wit, the balm of woe,
> The poor man's wealth, the prisoner's release,
> Th'indifferent judge between the high and low;
> With shield of proof shield me from out the prease
> Of those fierce darts Despair at me doth throw.
>
> (*Astrophel and Stella*, 39)

No study of the distribution of *proof, baiting, indifferent* or *darts* in present-day usage will of itself establish the co-ordinates by reference to which the effect necessary for an intelligent reading of this poem can be given to them. The appeal must be to the usage of the past whether extended into the present in the systematized and common form of a dictionary such as N.E.D., or in the reader's memory of similar contexts in the literature. In this latter case, much will depend on which contexts happen to have survived in the memory of a particular reader, and the field to which reference is made is much more individual than can be the case in questions of contemporary usage. An equally narrow base is provided by the selective process inherent in dictionary-making. Is sleep in the passage quoted thought of as a place in which wit is tortured, rested, or fished for? N.E.D. provides quotations from *King Henry VI* for bear-baiting, from as late as 1872 for resting-place and from 1708 for a fishing-place. Most present-day readers in my experience intuitively take the meaning of resting-place; I have not found one whose choice of this meaning was accompanied by an awareness of all three without the aid of the dictionary. It seems that the response is best thought of not as the result of the scanning of a field of usage, but as a response to the context (balm, etc.) and an assumption that the parallelism (not unlike that of Old English) as it were authorizes the required meaning. Whether the meaning will remain readily accessible in the future depends on the depth of the impression the poem makes on the reader, which in turn presumably depends in part at least on how clearly he understands it. An analogy to the existence in the vocabulary of readers of literature of words of this kind is the occurrence of heirloom objects in archaeological contexts. These may be found on the floor of a level later than that at which they were made, and their form and ornament may not be relatable to that of their present context and only to be understood in the context in which they were produced. It may even be that having been produced for one purpose in the service of some end they are re-used by subsequent generations for a different purpose in the service of a quite different end. A fragment originally everyday may by becoming an heirloom have acquired a special status and implication, like a fragment of a Roman glass jar treated as a jewel and re-set in a later Anglo-Saxon clay vessel.

Words in non-contemporary literature may be like this, as they are unlikely ever to be in present-day ordinary discourse. They may survive not as terms in a coherent series, amenable to modification by speakers and establishable by reference to them, but as the sole survivor, arbitrarily fixed when removed from its series, of a lost series only to be established by reference to past speakers. They may never in fact have been part of a series in a contemporary colloquial, any more than our knowledge of them in literature necessarily entitles us to use them in conversation (other than the academic conversation which conventionally includes all words in literary use, though it excludes many words in daily colloquial use). In any case our present knowledge of them is clearly based upon an immeasurably smaller range of contexts and varieties of syntactic role than is the case with most of our not exclusively literary vocabulary. We are very unlikely to be able instinctively to compare the relative frequencies of possible alternative interpretations, all possibilities are much more nearly equally likely and again a special sort of individual decision on our part is required. The particular immediate context is likely in these circumstances to have more than its usual influence.

I have for instance only one context for 'polyphiloprogenitive' so that my understanding of it owes as much to 'sapient sutlers of the Lord' as it does to analysis of its elements, and one might guess that most people used to reading literature written before this century are accustomed to accept words for which they have a comparatively very small number of contexts. And of course these people are a comparatively small portion of the English-speaking community, and have an untypically homogeneous experience.

Whilst this very narrow base of reference for some words in literature increases the need for individual effort on the reader's part it also increases the possibility of individual difference of response. However frequent a word's occurrences may have been in the eighteenth century, if only a dozen are in work at all read today, and one reader has encountered three of these and another reader only another three, there will naturally be a much greater possibility of difference in response than in contemporary discourse where the common shared occurrences run into thousands and the individual unshared ones are a minute percentage. In a difference of this kind we can only hope to favour the reading which is based upon contexts which happen to reflect those upon which the author based his value for the word, or contexts which happen to reflect the whole range of the word's usages and thus permit a choice from the correct material to be made.

How can we hope to do this? Appropriateness in the context may be one criterion, though of a fairly circular kind, but the definition of appropriateness here presents some difficulties. It must mean more than 'sense of a kind', for readers will quite rarely produce absolute nonsense as the interpretation of earlier literature, and failures are much more likely to be a matter of slightly missing the point than of producing something that could not possibly fit in. Appropriateness can only be 'the best sense bearing in mind the situation' and in this case, as distinct from ordinary discourse, we can only know the situation from the words. It is not independently present as an external check which serves initially to restrict the field of possible usage to be scanned, and subsequently to assure us that a correct choice has been made.

It thus appears that there are inherent in the situation of reading literature some problems, susceptible of description in linguistic terms of usage and context of situation, which are separate from and precedent to the questions with which interpretative, purely 'literary' criticism is concerned, and it seems likely that it is at this level that the difficulties of reading literature operate most decisively. For the linguistic abilities necessary to function effectively in common contexts of situation are not adequate to make a satisfactory reader of literature of the kind considered here, though they will serve for any literature that has restricted its demands so that it does not exceed them.

8

Linguistics and the Figures of Rhetoric

I

IF RHETORIC is an outmoded discipline, its influence lives on in the present-day study of literature at least in the 'figures of speech' (above all, metaphor) which form an important part of critical vocabulary. Neither the traditional 'definitions' of the rhetorical manuals, nor those of the more recent manuals of usage, provide a satisfactory account of these terms; and attempts to elucidate them by reference to the psychology or philosophy of language have met with only limited success, largely, it seems to me, because of the inadequacy of the linguistic part of the writers' explanatory equipment. In consequence, the subject of rhetorical figures has become an unjustifiably neglected department of literary education.

This chapter is not an attempt to provide a practical remedy for this state of affairs, in the form of detailed descriptions of figures of speech. (This last term is used in a loose modern sense, roughly incorporating all that was meant by 'figures of speech', 'tropes', and 'figures of thought' in classical rhetoric.)[1] Many of these figures (particularly those which traditionally belong under the heading 'figures of thought') appear to lie altogether outside the linguist's sphere of competency; others do not entirely fall

[1] See J. W. H. Atkins, *Literary Criticism in Antiquity*, vol. ii (Cambridge, 1934), pp. 18, 272. This and other volumes by Atkins document the history of rhetorical figures from their classical origin to the eighteenth century. More recent descriptions and exemplifications are to be found in Alexander Bain, *English Composition and Rhetoric*, enlarged edn., Part I (London, etc., 1887); and H. W. Fowler, *A Dictionary of Modern English Usage* (Oxford, 1926).

K

within it. Moreover, a consistent and accurate linguistic account of figures of speech can only be undertaken within the framework of a more general account of the characteristic linguistic features of literary texts. My primary aim, therefore, will be to suggest how linguistic theory can be accommodated to the task of describing such recurrent phenomena in literature as metaphor, parallelism, alliteration and antithesis.

Rhetoric only enters into the discussion in so far as it has provided us with most of our terminology for talking about these features. In a historical perspective, the *Ars Rhetorica* and *Ars Poetica* of classical tradition 'institutionalized' many of them, and combined with literary fashion to give special prominence to certain figures at certain historical periods. But my general concern is with characteristics of creative writing irrespective of author, period and language. It follows from this approach that such a question as 'How can we define a metaphor?' is, in a sense, misconceived: an unprejudiced examination of the recurrent linguistic features of literary texts may, or may not, yield a category which fits the traditional term 'metaphor' sufficiently well not to do violence to accepted usage. The terminology is logically subsequent to, not prior to, the system of classification.

II

By popular definition, literature is the creative use of language; and this, in the context of general linguistic description, can be equated with the use of unorthodox or deviant forms of language. It is not surprising that until recent years, linguistics contributed little to stylistic analysis: a discipline has to attain a degree of maturity and confidence before it can profitably take into its ken a type of material guaranteed to produce exceptions to rules of general application.

The essential prerequisite of the linguist's approach to literature is that he should have means to assign different degrees of generality to his statements about language. There are two particularly important ways in which the description of language entails generalization. In the first place, language operates by what may be called *descriptive* generalization, in the sense that a number of heterogeneous items A_1, A_2, A_3, A_4, . . . may be recognized as being in some sense 'the same thing', i.e. belonging to the same general category A. If the items *I*, *they*, *it*, etc., are given the generic grammatical name 'pronoun', this is because it is necessary to discern their likeness, despite grammatical differences such as the selection of a singular verb after *I* and a plural verb after *they*. A scale of *descriptive delicacy*[2] permits the grammarian to take account of the likeness or equivalence of linguistic items, whether in shape or function, whilst not neglecting, unless he so wishes, the differentiation to various degrees of refinement of items within general categories. Steps on this scale can be illustrated by the increasing delicacy of the grammatical classes 'pronoun': 'objective personal pronoun'; 'objective third-person pronoun'; 'objective third-person singular masculine non-reflexive pronoun'—the last class is of maximum delicacy, consisting of only one item (*him*). Any description of a language is relatively general and incomplete, or relatively detailed and complete, according to the depth of descriptive delicacy to which it penetrates.

The other type of generalization is implicit in the use of terms such as 'dialect' and 'language' (in the sense in which we talk of a particular language, such as English). The raw material for linguistic study is composed of numerous individual events of speaking, hearing, writing and reading; but it is assumed that from these events, generalizations can be made covering the linguistic behaviour of whole populations of large geographical areas. It is unfortunate that the word *language* commonly has to do service for at least three degrees of generalization, between which the linguist is bound to make a clear distinction. 'Language' (without the article) refers to the whole field of human behaviour which it is his task to study. 'A language' generally denotes a less general concept, convenient but in some cases arbitrarily defined, within which a particular linguistic enterprise or study is usually confined (e.g. English, Russian, Swahili). Further,

[2] Cf. M. A. K. Halliday, 'Categories of the theory of grammar', *Word*, xvii, 3 (1961), pp. 258–9, 272–3.

'language' is often used for a still less general aspect of linguistic behaviour, for example when it is said that 'Mr X speaks a different language from Mr Y.' (although both are Englishmen born and bred); 'Mr X uses one language to his wife, another to his employer'; or 'the inhabitants of St Ives, Cornwall, speak a different language from the inhabitants of Barnstaple, Devon'. If it is decided to make 'a language', such as English, the upper limit of generality for a particular description (as is generally the case), then the degrees of generality applying to different varieties of English can be plotted on a scale of increasing delicacy or differentiation, until such relative minutiae as 'the language Mr X uses in addressing his young daughter, aged 2' are taken into account. This type of delicacy, which may be entitled *institutional delicacy*,[3] operates on a scale which relates linguistic behaviour to other forms of social behaviour, and to the structure of society as composed of successively larger groupings of individuals and communities.

In fact it is more accurate to distinguish two scales of institutional delicacy. The first, the *register scale*,[4] handles various registers or roles of linguistic activity within society, distinguishing, for example, spoken language from written language; the language of respect from the language of condescension; the language of advertising from the language of science. The second distinguishes the linguistic habits of various sections of society, differentiated by age, social class, sex and geographical area. The end-point of this *dialect scale* is reached with the *idiolect*, or the aggregate of the characteristic linguistic habits of a particular individual within the linguistic community. The two scales can be visualized as intersecting axes; the literary works of a particular author, for instance, would have to be plotted, as a subject for linguistic study, with reference to both the register scale and the dialect scale.

These scales are not merely conveniences for the linguist's description, but reflect the nature of language itself. If we started

[3] The use of 'institutional' in this sense derives from Trevor Hill, 'Institutional Linguistics', *Orbis*, vii (1958), pp. 441–55.

[4] Following the use of 'register' by T. B. W. Reid ('Linguistics, Structuralism and Philology', *Archivum Linguisticum*, vii [1956], pp. 32 ff.) and others.

from the assumption that all differences in linguistic events are equally important, we would not only conclude that language is amorphous and incapable of systematic study, but would also be at a loss to explain how it acts as a vehicle of communication. Likenesses are more important than dissimilarities. Thus with reference to the dialect and register scales, it may be appropriate to study different varieties of English as if they were self-contained languages, before relating them in a total description of the language; but the fragmentation presupposes a synthesis.

It has been necessary to go at some length into the question of generality in language, in order to clarify the notion of *linguistic deviation* which is essential to a linguistic account of literary language. It is a commonplace that poets and other creative writers use language in unorthodox ways: that they are by convention allowed 'poetic licence'. But we also need to recognize *degrees* of unorthodoxy, and it is here that the scales of descriptive and institutional delicacy become relevant.

Degrees of deviation can initially be defined by reference to the scales of institutional delicacy. A linguistic feature will be highly deviant if it is unique to a low-generality variety of English; if it is common to a number of low-generality varieties, or unique to a variety of higher generality, it is to that extent less deviant. The least deviant, or 'most normal' feature of all will be that which is common to all varieties of English.

The scale of descriptive delicacy is brought in to assess the degree of structural importance of a feature which is institutionally deviant; or, in subjective terms, the degree of surprise it is capable of eliciting in the uninitiated reader (or listener). If in most varieties of English adverbial clauses beginning with *if* are distributed so that more *if* clauses precede than follow the main clauses on which they depend, whereas in one particular variety of English this tendency is reversed, this will constitute a relatively trivial deviation, identifiable only at a considerable depth of descriptive delicacy. A contrast to this is the frequently instanced case of the pronoun *thou/thee/thine/thy*, which is restricted to only a few varieties of English (e.g. religious English), and moreover represents a deviation of descriptive importance, involving a restatement of the systems of number and person, and the introduction of a new relation of concord (*thou canst*, etc.). In terms of social meaning, *thou* has a high 'strangeness value' or 'connotative value', being fraught with overtones of piety, historical period, 'poeticalness', and so forth.

A final word is necessary concerning the use of the word 'deviation'. This term has acquired a specific meaning with reference to a statistical norm, and it seems that this statistical use may well coincide, in practice, with the use adopted here. If it is imagined that a corpus of material has been selected to represent a variety of English at a given degree of institutional delicacy, and that this analysis has revealed two occurrences of the pronoun *thou* against 10,000 occurrences of the pronoun *you* in comparable conditions, the item *thou* will be statistically deviant. On increasing the depth of delicacy, the occurrences of *thou* would no doubt be found to coincide with a less general variety of the language: for example, if the original corpus was of educated spoken British English, the *thou*'s in question might well be found to occur in the language of strict Quakers, of Shakespeare quotation, or of the jocular simulation of a North Country dialect.

Now that a theoretical value has been assigned to the word 'deviation', we may proceed to a closer examination of its function in literary language. Literature is distinguished from other varieties of linguistic activity above all by the number and the importance of the deviant features it contains. The highly deviant character of these features is to be measured not only by the important degree of descriptive delicacy at which they operate, but in most cases, by an extreme lack of institutional generality. To all intents and purposes, the typical deviation in literary language can be considered unique to the text in which it occurs, and to this extent it resembles linguistic 'errors' and slips of the tongue, rather than such cases as the pronoun *thou*, which is associated with certain registers, and therefore has an accepted social meaning. This raises a descriptive problem. If literary English is viewed as a variety of English identified with reference to the register scale, how will its description fit into the total description of the language? A self-contained description of a 'literary language' would prove an impossible or at best an uninforming task. Since it would abound in unique deviations, it would be found to contain few of the restrictions on usage observed in other varieties of English, or at least whatever restrictions were perceived to exist through analysis of a working sample would be likely to evaporate on inspection of a further sample. In fact any corpus of material, however large, would be inadequate for a complete description of literary language: every new metaphor, for instance, would require an alteration of the existing description.

The difficulty of conceiving of a literary language as a describable language in its own right confirms the need to study it in the light of comparison with other varieties of the language; that is, chiefly in terms of linguistic deviation. This is not to suggest that literary language tends to amorphism: an individual text will be linguistically highly organized, but the features of organization (e.g. a recurrent lexical pattern carrying the symbolic theme of the work) will tend to be peculiar to that text, not general to literature as a whole. A linguistic analysis of a limited text, such as a poem, is indeed a practicable exercise; but this again presupposes comparison with other varieties of English.[5]

III

The adoption of an approach *via* general linguistic description has governed my choice of the adjective 'deviant' to characterize an essential (perhaps *the* essential) feature of literary language. This is unflattering to the creative writer, classing him with eccentrics, Mrs Malaprops, and anyone else who makes unorthodox or idiosyncratic use of language. Later we shall face the problem (crucial from the aesthetic point of view) of how to distinguish between a unique deviation which is meaningful and one which is merely an unmotivated aberration. But our immediate task is to exemplify and classify such deviations without respect to their artistic or other significance.

[5] Cf. M. A. K. Halliday, 'The Linguistic Study of Literary texts', *Preprints of the IXth International Congress of Linguists* (Cambridge, Mass., 1962), p. 197: 'Linguistic stylistics . . . is essentially a comparative study.'

An exceptionally bold linguistic device employed by Dylan Thomas has caught the attention of more than one linguist,[6] and will provide an illustrative starting-point. In phrases such as *all the sun long*, *a grief ago*, and *farmyards away* the deviation consists in an unrestricted choice of nouns (*farmyards, sun, grief*) in a position where normally only members of a limited list of nouns appear (in the last case, nouns of linear measurement such as *inches, feet, miles*). The effect of this is to upset the normal system of contrasts at this place in structure, and to substitute a new dual opposition between the deviant occurrence and the expected set.[7] The difference between the normal paradigm and the new *ad hoc* paradigm can be represented as follows:

NORMAL PARADIGM

inches	
feet	away
yards	
etc.	

NEW PARADIGM

inches	NORMAL	away
feet		
yards		
etc.		
farmyards	DEVIANT	

[6] E.g. S. R. Levin discusses *a grief ago* in 'Poetry and grammaticalness', *Preprints of the IXth International Congress of Linguists*, pp. 203–8.

[7] S. R. Levin (ibid., p. 206) suggests two other ways of accounting for a deviation such as this: (a) the deviant item is added on to the list of items ordinarily in contrast;

Here there is a clear division between 'deviant' and 'normal'. But for those aspects of linguistic organization where there are no closed lists of equivalent items, the distinction is relative: that is, between 'more deviant' and 'less deviant'. The deviation constitutes an unaccustomed extension of the range of choices, but not a disruption of established oppositions. Grammatical deviation is of this kind in the case of iterative structures. For example, the last verse of *This is the House that Jack Built* is a linguistic oddity in that it contains a long series of embedded relative clauses. Each verse after the first adds an extra clause, and represents a step in the direction of greater deviation; but it would be impossible to say at what point in this language-game deviation 'sets in'.

Lexical deviation, studied with reference to the frequency of collocations, or groups of lexical items in proximity,[8] is again a matter of gradience. One would have no hesitation in dubbing the collocation *damp smile* as deviant, but it would have to be placed on a scale of lesser-to-greater deviation on the lines of:

(1) broad smile (most normal)
(2) free smile
(3) damp smile
(4) high smile (most deviant)

Nevertheless, it appears that something akin to the direct contrast between deviation and normality postulated in the case of *farmyards away* is needed to account for the phenomenon of literary metaphor. In Edith Sitwell's phrase *fruitbuds that whimper*, *fruitbuds* occupies a position relative to *whimper* normally filled by a relatively homogeneous set of animate nouns *dog*, *cub*, *animal*, *child*, etc. This group of customary collocates might be said to constitute a 'collocational core' of items, such that an opposition

[8] For the place of collocation in linguistic study, see J. R. Firth, *Papers in Linguistics 1934–51* (London, 1957), pp. 194–5; and M. A. K. Halliday, 'Categories', p. 276.

---

and (*b*) a sub-class of nouns *containing* the deviant item (e.g. nouns of emotional state) is added to the list of items ordinarily in contrast. The explanation I offer is based on the principle that having diagnosed a violation of linguistic restraints, we have no grounds for supposing that the deviation implies further restraints (e.g. that it is a member of a 'class' of possible deviations including a *disappointment ago*, *a happiness ago*, etc., but not *a meal ago*, *a frost ago*, etc.).

is set up between the deviant collocation with *fruitbuds* and the total 'collocational core'. Hence from the viewpoint of literary appreciation, it is within the capability of metaphor (as opposed to simile) to suggest a connexion between the explicit *vehicle* (represented by the deviant item) and a less tangible cluster of associations constituting the *tenour* (and represented by the 'core' of customary collocations).[9] Other figurative uses of language can be better explained in terms of discrete grammatical oppositions. Contrasts such as personal/impersonal, animate/inanimate and concrete/abstract distinguish grammatical classes of nouns, and the use of an inanimate noun in a context appropriate to a personal noun, as in Milton's

> And caused the golden-tressed sun
> All the day long his course to run

is a type of deviation we recognize as *personification*. Other common metaphoric effects are produced by the substitution of a concrete for an abstract noun, or an animate for an inanimate noun.

The Czech term *aktualisace*, translated by Garvin as 'foregrounding', was used by the pre-war Prague school of linguistics in a sense roughly corresponding to my 'unique deviation'.[10] Deliberate linguistic 'foregrounding', according to the Prague linguists, is not confined to creative writing, but is also found, for example, in joking speech and children's language-games. Literature, however, is characterized by the 'consistency and systematic character of foregrounding'.[11] The metaphorical term 'foreground' suggests the figure/ground opposition of gestalt psychology: the patterns of normal language are relevant to literary art only in providing a 'background' for the structured deployment of deviations from the norm. If the gestalt metaphor is retained, the word 'figures' of 'figures of speech' is reanimated

[9] The terms *tenour* and *vehicle* are borrowed from I. A. Richards, *Philosophy of Rhetoric* (New York and London, 1936), pp. 96 ff.

[10] See Paul L. Garvin, trans., *A Prague School Reader on Esthetics, Literary Structure and Style* (*Publications of the Washington Linguistic Club* I, Washington, 1958), esp. B. Havránek, 'The functional differentiation of the standard language', pp. 1–18.

[11] J. Mukarovský, 'Standard language and poetic language', ibid., p. 23.

by a technical pun. There is no need, however, to explore the psychological implications of the analogy. 'Figures', in the sense of deviant or foregrounded features of literary language, are observable and classifiable features of texts; how they register on the mind is beyond the scope of linguistic study, and irrelevant to the present stage of the discussion.

Figures can be initially classified as either *syntagmatic* or *paradigmatic*. An elementary distinction is often made between these two complementary aspects of linguistic patterning: items are associated syntagmatically when they combine sequentially in the chain of linguistic events, and paradigmatically when they enter into a system or set of possible selections at one point in the chain. The distinction is conventionally indicated in grammars by horizontal and vertical presentation on the printed page; for example, clause elements in chain relation are represented *Subject-Verb-Complement*, etc., whereas case-endings in choice relation are shown by vertical display in the declension of a Latin noun. Types of figure illustrated so far have been paradigmatic: they have consisted in the selection of an item which is not a member of the normal range of choices available at its place in the linguistic chain. In other words, where there is a choice between equivalent items, the writer chooses one which is not equivalent to (i.e. in contrast to) the normal range of choices. Syntagmatic foregrounding results from the opposite process: where there is choice to be made at different points in the chain, the writer repeatedly makes the same selection. This, in Jakobson's words, is the projection of 'the principle of equivalence from the axis of selection into the axis of combination.'[12] A syntagmatic figure introduces a layer of patterning additional to those normally operating within the language; for example, in an alliterative figure such as *the furrow followed free* (S. T. Coleridge), the selection of the same initial phoneme /f/ on successive accented syllables imposes a repetitive pattern ($\overset{\times}{-}\ \acute{f}\ \overset{\times}{-}\ \acute{f}\ \overset{\times}{-}\ \acute{f}$) which in other types of discourse would be fortuitous and of no communicative value. The notion of figure-and-ground may again be

[12] Roman Jakobson, 'Linguistics and poetics', Thomas A. Sebeok, ed., *Style in Language* (New York, 1960), p. 358.

useful in furnishing a visual analogue of the two types of foregrounding:

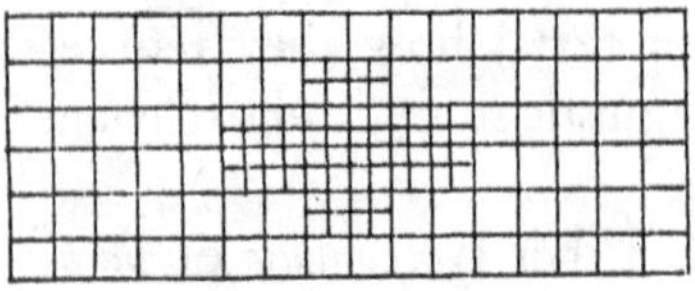

Syntagmatic Figure

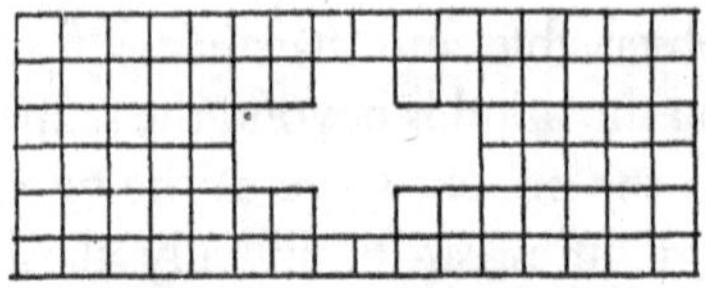

Paradigmatic Figure

The syntagmatic figure can be imagined as a pattern superimposed on the background of ordinary linguistic patterning; the paradigmatic figure as a gap in the established code—a violation of the predictable pattern.

Our understanding of the term 'foregrounding' should, of course, accommodate both the discrete and the relative types of deviation. The latter category is applicable to syntagmatic, as well as paradigmatic figures. A syntagmatic figure may be thought of as a realization, to a greater or lesser degree, of the potential syntagmatic regularity of a language. A trivial degree of regularity is present in the repetition of the verb+object construction (a weak form of parallelism) in

He found his key and opened the door.

However, as the clause with a direct object is very common in English, the general probability of such a pattern is in any case fairly high. In contrast, the two clauses in Othello's

I kissed thee ere I killed thee

exhibit a high order of syntagmatic correspondence. Apart from identity of structure (subject+verb+object), the second clause echoes the first in containing identical pronouns (*I*, *thee*) and an identical morpheme (*-ed*) in equivalent syntactic positions. This formal pattern is further reinforced at the phonological level in the initial phonemic correspondence of *kissed* and *killed*.

With the syntagmatic category, a further important division is to be made between *schematic* and *prosodic* foregrounding. The preceding examples of syntagmatic figures have illustrated the former; the latter is the type of syntagmatic regularity that distinguishes verse from prose literature. The most satisfactory criterion by which they may be distinguished is this: prosodic foregrounding, although deviant in respect of general linguistic norms, is itself a norm for the type of text (a poem) in which it functions.[13] Hence the phenomenon of defeated expectancy in verse: a failure of the predicted prosodic foregrounding to materialize constitutes a deviation from the secondary, or textual norm.

IV

Further consideration need not be given to prosodic foregrounding, which is outside our subject, nor to the subtleties of its delimitation in different languages, cultures, and literary modes.[14] The next step is a further linguistic classification of paradigmatic and schematic figures.

We distinguish, in the first place, between the different levels of linguistic function at which a figure is to be identified and described. On this basis, a figure is classified as formal (grammatical or lexical), phonological, orthographic, or semantic (referential or contextual),[15] or perhaps assigned to a combination of these categories. For example, alliteration, rhyme, vowel-harmony and assonance (where these are not prosodic phenomena) are *phonological* schematic figures, all consisting in an adscititious regularity of phonematic sequences. Parallelism, anaphora, and many of the schemes distinguished in Renaissance rhetoric (such as antistrophe and epanalepsis)[16] are *formal* schematic figures, consisting in an adscititious regularity of various types of formal patterning. In distinguishing between these various

[13] This amounts to the same as saying, with S. R. Levin in *Linguistic Structures in Poetry* (*Janua Linguarum* XXIII, The Hague, 1962), that 'many features distinguishing poetry from ordinary discourse result from the mere fact that a writer addresses himself to writing a poem' (p. 59).

[14] See J. Lotz, 'Metric Typology' in Sebeok, op. cit., pp. 135–48.

[15] On Linguistic levels see J. R. Firth, 'Modes of meaning' in *Papers in Linguistics*, pp. 190–215, and M. A. K. Halliday, 'Categories', pp. 243–4.

[16] See, for example, George Puttenham's seven figures of 'repetition' in *The Arte of English Poesie*, ed. Gladys D. Willcock and Alice Walker (Cambridge, 1936), pp. 198–202.

types, it is important to stipulate the degree of abstraction at which the pattern is recognized. Highly abstract grammatical patterns, such as clause structures expressed in terms of subject, verb, complement, etc., often form the basis of a schematic figure which is manifested in a more specific regularity. Thus the parallelism of Goldsmith's

> Where wealth accumulates, and men decay

does not consist only in the repetition of like clause structures (subject+verb), but in the fact that in each case the clause elements have single words as their exponents (*wealth, accumulates, men, decay*). A more highly organized schematic pattern will extend to a regularity at the most specific level of formal patterning: a repetition of individual formal items such as *my*, *for* and *a* in the following passage from *Richard II*:

> I'll give my jewels for a set of beads,
> My gorgeous palace for a hermitage,
> My gay apparel for an almsman's gown,
> My figured goblets for a dish of wood,
> My sceptre for a palmer's walking staff,
> My subjects for a pair of carved saints,
> And my large kingdom for a little grave,
> A little, little grave, an obscure grave.

Anaphora, at least in H. W. Fowler's sense (marked repetition of a word or a phrase in successive clauses or sentences)[17] operates predominantly on the plane of individual formal (lexical or grammatical) items. In David's lament for his son

> O my son Absalom, my son, my son Absalom! Would God I had died for thee, O Absalom, my son, my son!
>
> (II Samuel)

the repetition of individual sequences of words is more significant than the grammatical parallelism which accompanies it.

A comparison of formal and phonological schematic figures reveals that we cannot always handle the different linguistic levels in isolation from one another. The presence of formal

[17] Entry in *A Dictionary of Modern English Usage.*

schematic patterning to some extent implies the presence of phonological schematic patterning (i.e. to repeat a word is to repeat the sounds of which it is composed). Hopkins's extensive use of anaphora appears to be one with his deployment of phonological schemes. The lexical repetitions in his lines:

> My aspens dear, whose airy cages quelled,
> Quelled or quenched in leaves the leaping sun,
> All felled, felled, are all felled
>
> (*Binsey Poplars*)

contribute to the effects produced by alliteration, rhyme and vowel harmony. But the dependence is not reciprocal: phonological repetitions (e.g. the repetition of /li/ in *leaves* and *leaping*) may be independent of formal correspondences.

Another type of dependency exists between formal paradigmatic and semantic foregrounding. We have already noted that figurative meaning is expressed by some kind of formal deviation, whether in the selection of an inappropriate grammatical class or in the collocational foreground of a lexical item. Nevertheless, the figurative/literal dichotomy is primarily a matter of referential semantics. The term 'figurative' implies that an item has been given a referential meaning outside its normal range of meanings (as listed, for example, in a dictionary entry). A sober re-reading of a well-known passage from Bacon

> Some books are to be tasted, others to be swallowed, and some few to be chewed and digested
>
> (*Of Studies*)

will show that by the standards of the accepted code (i.e. 'literal meaning') a literary metaphor is a semantic absurdity. Our dictionaries are full, however, of metaphorical meanings which in the course of linguistic history have lost their deviant character ('dead metaphors').

At least three kinds of semantic foregrounding can be signalled by deviant collocation. In Hopkins's

> Then let the march tread our ears
>
> (*At the Wedding March*)

the collocation of *tread* and *ears*, like that of *books* and *tasted*, etc., in Bacon's apophthegm, is a juxtaposition of semantic incompatibles—the linguistic basis of metaphor. Antonymy is a special case of semantic incompatibility; when Milton's Samson collocates *living* and *death*:

> To live a life half-dead, a living death

he produces a particular type of semantic absurdity we recognize as paradox or oxymoron. This line also illustrates, in the collocation of *live* and *life*, a third kind of oddity: a pleonasm, or semantic redundancy consisting in the combination of synonymous items. The verse from Ecclesiastes

> I praise the dead which are already dead more than the living which are yet alive

contains two more obvious examples of this type of foregrounding.

After the description of figures by the linguistic levels at which they function, an obvious next stage in the analysis is to classify them according to relevant features of organization within each level. For instance, to the preceding examples of parallelism of clause structure we may add an example of parallelism of nominal phrase structure, Pope's

> A tim'rous friend and a suspicious foe
> (*Epistle to Dr Arbuthnot*)

(a+Adjective+Noun, a+Adjective+Noun). In calling this 'a different kind' of parallelism from the others, we call into play the ordinary descriptive categories of English grammar. But in fully accounting for possible varieties of formal parallelism on these lines, we would need to specify (*a*) the largest grammatical unit entering into the structural equivalence (e.g. sentence, clause, phrase, etc.); (*b*) the degree of identity of the class exponents of the elements of structure (e.g. whether they are both nouns, animate nouns, personal nouns, etc.); and (*c*) the extent to which the structural elements have identical exponents at lower ranks (the maximum similarity here would be complete identity of formal items, which would also imply complete identity under (*b*)). A similar type of classification might be made of paradigmatic figures. As the number of distinctions that can be made on the basis of linguistic categories is virtually boundless, we have to decide on the amount of detail we wish our classification to include.

Schematic figures can be further analysed abstractly as configurations of foregrounded regularities: that is, as patterns in their own right, without reference to the 'background' of normal linguistic patterning. In its simplest manifestation, a schematic figure is a pattern consisting of two equivalent phases or segments, representable as *aa* (or *a—a—* if they are separated by a sequence of unforegrounded material). Although there is no clear limitation on the number of phases in a schematic pattern, in literature the pattern which is simplest in this respect seems also to be the most important: a symptom of this is our preference for a separate critical term (balance) for a parallelism consisting of two phases only. All the parallelisms so far quoted have been binary, excepting the passage from *Richard II*, which has the structure *aaaaaaa*. Elizabethan stage rhetoric, in fact, provides examples of a more complex type of configuration, in which there is an alternation of two or more sets of equivalent phases:

> He spake me fair, this other gave me strokes:
> He promised life, this other threatened death:
> He won my life, this other conquered me . . .

This schematic pattern from *Spanish Tragedy* has the structure *ababab*. There is yet the further possibility that two phases may be in a symmetrical relation, such that the second is in some sense the mirror image of the first. The placing of equivalent formal items in Hamlet's line

> What's Hecuba to him, or he to Hecuba

yields the formula *abccba*, and an analogous configuration of grammatical elements defines the rhetorical figure *chiasmus*. Such dimensions of description need to be recognized, although their relevance to literary appreciation is perhaps marginal, and their potential complexities are more fully realized in prosodic than in schematic foregrounding.

A linguistic classification of literary figures such as that outlined above can proceed from the most general distinctions towards the most specific; but the only complete classification would be that which gave a separate characterization of each unique deviation. Quintilian was justified in complaining that the practice of enumerating figures of speech was an overestimated pastime among rhetoricians:[18] the inventory of such figures is potentially infinite. Whereas linguistics provides the technique for pursuing this classification to the point of boredom, it also provides a criterion (in the scale of descriptive delicacy) for deciding which are the most significant (least trivial) distinctions.

V

I return finally to the question which looms over the gap between linguistic analysis and critical appreciation. When is a unique deviation meaningful, and when is it merely a piece of nonsense? In one sense, the first part of this question is a contradiction in terms: a broad definition of meaningfulness equates it with the appropriate use of linguistic conventions. Similarly, if we want to find a technical definition of nonsense, none will suit it better than 'that which contravenes the established rules of the language.' From this point of view, therefore, poetry is a variety of nonsense (as, indeed, it is to some people). But another interpretation of 'nonsense' might be 'language that communicates nothing'; and it must be admitted that this 'nonsense' is virtually a fiction. Even a linguistic error or aberration communicates something: to write *authoritis* for *arthritis*, for example, might be to convey to your reader that you are unfamiliar with the language, a bad speller, or the kind of semi-educated person who commits malapropisms. It is in this wider sense of meaningfulness that literary foregrounding communicates. Nevertheless, we must hasten to distinguish between the 'significant deviations' of

[18] See J. W. H. Atkins, *Literary Criticism in Antiquity*, vol. ii, p. 273.

literary language, and unmotivated deviations which have a trivial and unintended meaning.

The approach to this problem of 'significance' depends very much on whether paradigmatic or schematic foregrounding is under consideration. The former, it has been suggested, constitutes a disruption, at one particular level, of the normal patterns of linguistic organization. The gap can be filled, and the deviation rendered meaningful, only if some latent relation (linguistic or non-linguistic) implied in the nature of the deviation compensates for the missing overt linguistic relation. We may speak of the latent connexion by which we interpret a paradigmatic deviation as its *warranty*, implying that the connexion is a positive requirement if sense is to be made of the linguistic event as a whole. But in the case of schematic foregounding, the normal functions of the language are undisturbed, and the total linguistic event is meaningful even if the deviation is unmotivated (as it might be in an adventitious alliteration such as *Tell Tom it's tea-time*). It is more fitting to refer to the interpretative connexion of a schematic figure as its *reinforcement*: we do not have to make good a deficiency, but to explain a superfluity of patterning. The medieval labels for schemes and tropes, *ornatus facilis* and *ornatus difficilis*, are perhaps a reflection of the nature of the difference between these processes.

One kind of warranty for a paradigmatic figure is a connexion established at some other level of linguistic function. The morphological extravagances of *Finnegan's Wake* (e.g. *wholeborrow*, *Gracehoper*) are interpreted in the light of their phonological resemblance to established words in the language (*wheelbarrow*, *grasshopper*). Most examples of word-play are to be explained in terms of a phonological compensation (homonymy or partial homonymy) for formal deviation. Another kind of warranty consists in the preservation of a prosodic pattern: the need for a rhyme or for metrical regularity supplies a motive (aesthetically dubious) for a foregrounded arrangement of grammatical elements. This type of grammatical foregrounding, for which the rhetorical term 'hyperbaton' is available, may also contribute to a schematic figure. In Francis Thompson's *The Hound of Heaven*:

Yea, faileth now even dream
The dreamer, and the lute the lutanist

the transposition of the clause elements out of their normal affirmative order into verb+adjunct+subject+object upholds the parallelism of *dream the dreamer* and *lute the lutanist.*

No linguistic warranty can be found for metaphor: instead, the compensatory connexion is to be sought outside language, in some kind of psychological, emotional or perceptual relation between the literal and figurative meanings of the item(s) concerned. In the line from Donne's *The Apparition*

Then thy sick taper will begin to wink

the deviant items *sick* and *wink* become meaningful on the recognition of appropriate analogies—between someone who is ill and a candle which is burning out, and between the intermittent light of a candle and the winking of an eye. In probing more deeply into the meaning of these metaphors, we attach further significance to them in the light of the total symbolic context of the poem. A similar type of semantic deviation in *Humphrey Clinker* has a very different kind of extra-linguistic warranty:

> Hark ye, Clinker, you are a most notorious offender. You stand convicted of sickness, hunger, wretchedness and want.

The juxtaposition of semantic incompatibles here leads to the equation 'crime = misfortune', an absurdity which gains its point through ironic interpretation.

The linguistic/non-linguistic distinction also applies to the reinforcement of schematic figures. The Biblical

Absent in body, but present in spirit
(I Corinthians)

exemplifies a marked form of antithesis in which parallelism is reinforced by antonymy; i.e. by a linguistic connexion at the level of referential semantics. The phases of the schematic figure establish an equivalence between *absent* and *present*, *body* and *spirit*, and this relationship in each case corresponds to a systemic semantic contrast.[19] The parallelism of *I kissed thee ere I killed thee*, on the other hand, has no linguistic reinforcement. The two words equivalent in respect of the pattern, *kissed* and *killed*, are in no easily definable semantic relationship; their antithetic reinforcement comes rather from emotive contrast and from the dramatic context. The reinforcement of phonological schemes may be found in their contribution to figures at other levels. Alliteration, for example, underlines the grammatical parallelism of Marlowe's

> Of conquer'd kingdoms and of cities sack'd
> (1 *Tamberlaine*)

and the paradox of Shakespeare's

> So foul and fair a day I have not seen.
> (*Macbeth*)

In other cases, we look for a non-linguistic connexion: some kind of imitative connexion between the sound pattern and other extralinguistic implications of the text, such as is suggested by the final sibilants of Keats's

> Thou watchest the last oozings hours by hours.
> (*To Autumn*)

Of all reinforcements, such onomatopoeic effects are perhaps the least accessible to study.

The discussion of non-linguistic warranty and reinforcement has brought us beyond the bounds of linguistic study, although for the critic it is perhaps the most important aspect of the study of figures of speech. Linguistic warranty and reinforcement account for only the most obvious effects of literary language: the kind of effects which explain the point of a linguistic game or joke, but in literary explication only serve to point the way to further relevant non-linguistic connexions. The conclusion is not surprising: that the most interesting and illuminating

[19] The importance in poetry of such phenomena as this is discussed by Levin (*Linguistic Structures and Poetry*, pp. 30 ff.) under the heading of 'coupling'. The distinction I make between *Absent in body, but present in spirit* and *I kissed thee ere I killed thee* presupposes a structural approach to referential semantics which Levin, in common with many other linguists, does not entertain.

aspect of communication in literature is beyond the scope of linguistics. The literary writer's object, after all, is to transcend the limitations of ordinary language, and this is the real sense in which he can be said to use language creatively. But meaning in literature cannot be studied without constant reference to the observable patterns of language, and I have attempted to show to what extent linguistics can contribute to this study, by describing and classifying the mechanisms of deviation which are basic to the creative use of language.[20]

[20] (Editor's note). Since this chapter was written there has been published *Proceedings of the IXth International Congress of Linguists*, ed. H. G. Lunt (The Hague, 1964). See notes 5, 6, 7 above, and ch. 4 note 2. There are some slight differences from the originally available *Preprints*.

9
Chaucer's Epistolary Style

IN THIS ESSAY there would seem to be little point in adopting a rigid set of analytical terminology. It is an exercise in sympathy, asking about historical conditions questions which inevitably demand of the inquirer the art of relation. Analysis developed chiefly from assumptions about the nature of language tends to assume a timeless human imagination. Concerning persons and events of relatively short age in our own lifetimes, we know such a view to over-simplify when it seems most to complicate. Often such methodology lends a completed linguistic logic to a more than literary *inconscience*. I have tried to draw out of Chaucer's writing evidence for his reading and use of a particular literary genre, the verse epistle. If the study begins in a narrow, descriptive channel, yet it is hoped that through the necessity of providing connexions between many kinds of evidence the developing view will have emerged as wider, more complex and more humane.

If one were to attempt to reconstruct Chaucer's attitude to the verse epistle where would one begin? Most obviously, with the remains of the Ovidian heroic epistle embodied in the *Legend of Good Women* and with the two letters incorporated in Book V of *Troilus and Criseyde*. Less obviously, one might begin with the *Envoi a Scogan* or *a Bukton*.

The fragments of the *Heroides* in the *Legend* tell us little or nothing about Chaucer's feeling for the Ovidian heroic epistle.

Here the total epistolary format has been abandoned and the heroine's words or quotation of Ovid conform more or less to the narrative lament pattern common to Dido in Book I of the *Hous of Fame* and Criseyde in Books II and IV of *Troilus*. Chaucer did not have to rearrange much, for the epistolary texture of the *Heroides* lies mainly in an opening formula approximating to ordinary Roman letter-writing usage: where the writer and the recipient are identified and the primary occasion for writing is mentioned:

> Hospita, Demophoon, tua te Rhodopeia Phyllis
> ultra promissum tempus abesse queror.
> (*Heroides*, II. 1–2)

Although Ovid rings many changes on this formula he occasionally omits it. Compare Medea to Jason:

> At tibi Colchorum, memini, regina vacavi,
> ars mea cum peteres ut tibi ferret opem.
> (*Heroides*, XII. 1–2)

In each case the conclusion of the heroic epistle lacks any stylistic reference to a letter-writing convention of 'signing off'. Thus, the dramatic quality of Ovid's verse is only loosely connected with a letter form. Essentially, the *Heroides* are theatrical *suasoriae*. Chaucer has merely carried the liberation a stage further to suit his own narrative requirements.

In the letters in *Troilus* V, some trouble has been taken to create an epistolary impression. In the case of Troilus's letter (ll. 1317–421) there is an exordium formula where the writer identifies himself (in terms of his function as lover and 'servant' which he imagines, mistakenly, to be unique to him) employing the 'I recommend myself to you' form of opening address.[1] The letter also uses a signing off device common to classical and medieval usage:

> And far now wel, myn owen swete herte.

Apart from these touches, the content of the letter is stylistically indistinct from any of the 'nounal', phraseological verse belong-

[1] Cf. Norman Davis, *Paston Letters* (Oxford, 1958), nos. 1–5, 7, 8, 10, 11, etc., for this formula in ordinary use.

ing to the amatory complaint genre.[2] Criseyde's letter (ll. 1590–631) also makes use of an opening formula: 'I send you health', and identifies the recipient (but, significantly, not the writer):

> How myght a wight in torment and in drede
> And heleless, you sende as yet gladnesse?

The letter ends with the same farewell *topos*. Subscriptions and signatures accompany the letters (*Le vostre T* and *La Vostre C*) in some MSS but not in others.[3] Given the normal rime-royal pattern of the poem these touches cannot derive from Chaucer *ipse* but must have been incorporated from scribal marginalia.

Chaucer's polite, graceful and conventional style in these letters sets the tone for the vast number of amatory verse epistles which was to be written in England in the fifteenth century.[4] Incidentally, Chaucer's letter style closely resembles that of two verse epistles writen by Deschamps to ladies of his acquaintance, balades MCCXLIV and MCCXLV.[5] These letters are formally *balades* in three stanzas with refrain plus *envoi* and refrain. They are really 'balades en manière de lettre'. Deschamps's manner in these two balade letters does not correspond to his usual epistolary style reserved for more intimate exchanges.[6] The intimate verse letters are long rambling affairs poured out in enumerative octosyllabic couplets. The style is similar in Latin and French. They are racy, unsophisticated and crammed with detail. Opening, closing and dating formulae are the rule:

> Et Dieux qui tous biens fait et donne,
> Vous puist telement ordonner,
> Qu'en la fin vous vueille donner
> Son saint regne qui pas ne fine,

[2] Cf. Emrys Jones, *Surrey: Poems* (Oxford, 1964), p. xxiii.

[3] MSS *Cp*, *J*, *S1* (*Le Vostre T*); *H1*, *D*, *S1*, *S2*, (*La Vostre C*) include. The rest omit.

[4] Cf. Rossell Hope Robbins, *The Index of Middle English Verse* (New York, 1943), p. 753 for a list. The list requires revision, however. Some items are not epistles whilst other possible items have been missed out.

[5] *Œuvres Completes* (*S.A.T.F.* Paris, 1878–), VII, pp. 122–5.

[6] Cf. MCCCLVIII to Radulphus Vitardus (VII, 128–31); Lettres MCCCCVI–MCCCCXXI (VIII, 3–73). The best example, perhaps, of this kind of verse in English is the first 27 lines of Dunbar's comic 'Dirige' which are in the Deschampsian epistle style (cf. James Kinsley, *William Dunbar: Poems* [Oxford, 1958], pp. 98–9).

Si vray que j'eusse en la cuisine
Au jour d'uy voluntiers esté
De mon frere d'umilité,
Delez vous touz pour vous servir,
Si j'en peusse avoir loisir!
Et mauditte soit mon assise
Par qui je pers mon entreprise!
Escript a la Ferté Alès
Ou il n'a que frommaige et lès
Et IIII causes seulement,
Pur vin et mauvais logement,
Ce deuisisme jour de decembre,
En une reumatique chambre.[7]

Although medieval manuals existed for the writing of actual letters,[8] the various poetry manuals contain little about verse epistles. Rhetorically, at least, the genre simply did not exist as a distinct formal unit. In practice, medieval Latin poets cultivated the form after the Ovidian distichs of the *Tristia* and the *Ex Ponto*.[9] Although these poets of the eleventh and twelfth centuries wrote about intimate things, their style is thoroughly Ovidian: polished, epigrammatic, learned and full of mythological ornament. There is nothing of the easy, refined Horatian *sermo* in their style.

If we bear in mind the Ovidian preoccupations of the French medieval Latin poets, the 'balade' and the octosyllabic 'scribbling' style of Deschamps, it is surprising to see none of this reflected in Chaucer's two genuine, independent, poetic epistles, the *Envoi a Scogan* and the *Envoi a Bukton*.[10] Perhaps equally surprising is

[7] Lettre MCCCCXIX, ll. 94–110 (VIII, p. 66): 'A mes Seigneurs de la Chambre de Comptes, disans en l'Ostel de Sire Guillaume Brunel, Tresorier de France'.

[8] Cf. those quoted by C. S. Baldwin, *Medieval rhetoric and poetic to 1400* (Gloucester, Mass., 1959), pp. 212–27.

[9] Matthew of Vendome, Hildebert of Lavardin, Baudry of Bourgueil, Godfrey of Reims, Radulf of Tartarius. Of these, Radulf is, perhaps, the most Ovidian.

[10] The title 'L'Envoi' is normally interpreted to mean 'a poem in balade measure having an *envoie* as a concluding stanza' (*MED*). The poem to Scogan is cited as an example of the *sb.* in this sense. *Scogan* is not in balade measure. 'L'Envoi' here means 'a letter', as the Latin subtitling in the Camb. Univ. Lib. MS Gg. 4.27 ('Litera de Scogon per G.C.') indicates. Baugh, *Chaucer's Major Poetry* (London, 1964), p. 538 correctly identifies the poem as a 'verse epistle.'

that stylistically these poems bear no resemblance to the Letters of Troilus and Criseyde which so completely came to dominate later exercises in the verse epistle in England.

Although the two letters (especially the *Envoi a Scogan*) are remarkably independent of poetic models yet it is valuable to ask if either or both can be related to any previous poems. The *Envoi a Bukton* has been compared (unsuccessfully) by Brusendorff and Kittredge to some of Deschamps's Balades.[11] The most striking imagery of the *Envoi a Scogan* (ll. 38 ff.) has been linked by Professor Robinson with Alan of Lille's prose and verse prefaces to the *Anticlaudianus;* this same imagery has been associated with Ovid's *Tristia*, V. XII. 21 ff. by Kittredge.[12] Chaucer's lines (36–40):

> Nay, Scogan, say not so, for I m'excuse—
> God helpe me so—in no rym, dowteles,
> Ne thynke I never of slep to wake my muse
> That rusteth in my shethe stille in pees.
> While I was yong, I put hir forth in prees;

cannot be linked with either Alan or Ovid. The image which is most pertinent in Alan (*Prologus* 3):

> Ne iaceat calamus scabra rubigine torpens

really turns on the notion of the 'reed pen' as 'rusty' in the way that grain neglected or unused lies 'mildewed'. The image is developed in line 6: *et in tenui lasciuit harundine musa* ('and the muse sings in the thin reed'). Ovid's lines:

> adde quod ingenium longa rubigine læsum
> torpet et est multo, quam fuit ante, minus.

> ('Besides, my talent, injured by long neglect,
> is dull, much inferior to what it was before')

do not properly contain a physical image. 'Robigo' in the passage has, in effect, an abstract force. Moreover, the operative element

[11] Cf. A. Brusendorff, *The Chaucer Tradition* (Copenhagen, 1925), p. 487; G. L. Kittredge, *MLN* xxiv, p. 14 ff.

[12] Cf. F. N. Robinson, *The Works of Geoffrey Chaucer*, Second Edition, (London, 1957), p. 863.

in Chaucer's imagery is not so much 'rust' as the underlying metaphor of the pen = sword. The verbal basis of the image derives partly from the Latin *sb. stylus* which meant either a 'pen' or a 'dagger'.[13] But the complex use of this image reflected in ll. 36–40 is derived from Horace, *Satires*, II. ll. 39–44, a hitherto unsuspected source:[14]

> Sed hic stylus haud petet ultro
> quenquam animantem; et me veluti custodiet ensis
> vagina tectus; . . .
> . . . O pater et rex
> Juppiter, ut pereat positum rubigine telum,
> Nec quisquam noceat cupido mihi pacis!

(But this pen of mine shall not willfully attack any man breathing; and shall defend me like a sword that is sheathed in the scabbard; . . . O Jupiter, father and sovereign, may my weapon laid aside wear away with rust, and may no one injure me, who am desirous of peace!)

The fundamental force of the image in the Horatian passage (and in most of the examples cited in footnote 13) is that a pen is like a sword when it is employed in writing criticism or satiric verses. Baugh's paraphrase of Chaucer's lines is incomplete:

> As for me, my muse is rusting in its sheath. There was a time when this wasn't so, but all things pass away.[15]

Chaucer has been jestingly exposing and castigating Scogan for his failure to maintain good faith in his recent love-affair. He adds that Cupid will have his revenge on the middle-aged. The author then suggests that Scogan is saying to himself 'the old goat is amusing himself in a bit of mocking verse'. Chaucer's

[13] Cf. similar uses of this ambiguity in Cicero, *Philippicae*, 2.14.34 *Oratio pro Cluento*, 44.123; Pliny, *Epistulae*, 7.9.7; Ovid, *Epistulae ex Ponto*, IV.XIV.20. Chaucer's use of the image is more compressed in that he uses no concrete *sb.* to refer to the pen. He allows the physical association of 'shethe' and 'rusteth' with 'muse' to create the traditional sense.

[14] This Horatian passage is not quoted by John of Salisbury in the *Polycraticus* or the *Metalogicon* nor does it seem to have been imitated by medieval Latin poets. It does not occur in any medieval *florilegia* of Horace that I have seen. It is perhaps valuable in proving that Chaucer knew Horace.

[15] Op cit., p. 538.

reply amounts to a playful, depreciating denial that he is willing or able to write verse—verse of a particular kind, verse that is capable of hurting.[16] After all, the poem humorously chides Scogan for his lack of faith towards his mistress and the *envoi* makes it clear that Scogan is also neglecting his friend Chaucer. The poem ends with the warning never to 'defy Love again'—or to neglect Chaucer. The reworking of the Horatian passage implies that Chaucer is at once assuring Scogan that he is not really 'getting at him' and suggesting that the aged, neglected Chaucer in this poem has a hit or two left in his sword. Chaucer's ambiguous blend of playfulness and seriousness is typically Horatian. And this brings us to the dominant style of the epistle. It is not 'courtly', nor 'Ovidian' but 'Horatian'. The borrowed Horatian passage and imagery keynote the prevailing artistic mode. One of the most important elements in the Horatian epistle and satire was its easy, urbane, conversational tone.[17] Chaucer has in this poem and in the *Envoi a Bukton* tried to capture the easy, conversational style of the Horatian epistle. It is difficult to prove conclusively that the poem should convey this impression. The following combination of factors probably contributes to an urbane, conversational effect: (1) the large amount of syntactic enjambment combined with a consistent use of inversions and suspensions which suggests intelligence and sophistication. There is a marked absence of implied verse units in terms of single line lengths. At least two stanzas are one continuous, developing period; (2) the marked absence of final, 'inflexional' syllables (*-e*, *-es*) pronounced for metrical value. In 49 lines there are only 10 possible cases. The balance has been shifted from syllabic consciousness towards a purely accentual tendency without any disruption of the iambic smoothness of the rhythm. Sense naturally is supported by stress; (3) a complete absence of verse tags or fillers; (4) a complete absence of 'poetic' 'fine amour' terms (e.g. *smerte*, *intent*, *servise*, *pain*, *proof*, *stedfastnes*, etc.) in a context where such terms might be expected. In line

[16] For example, the phrase 'putte forth in prees' in this context does not mean 'to compete' (Robinson) but 'to offer battle' (cf. *The Former Age*, l. 33).

[17] Cf. E. Fraenkel, *Horace* (Oxford, 1959), pp. 309, 399.

44 the nouns *grace* ('power to bestow favours'), *honour* and *worthyness* refer to the values of φιλοτιμία not to the courtly values of φιληδονία.

While the syntax, imagery and tone of the poem imitate Horace's satires and epistles, the structure is not typical of these Horatian genres. The poem's structure is indirect and disproportionate.[18] The whole poem, with the exception of the *envoi*, rebukes Scogan elaborately for his cowardly behaviour towards a woman. It is only in the *envoi* that the 'real' subject emerges: Chaucer, in unrewarded obscurity in Greenwich, reminds Scogan, at court at Windsor, that Cicero in the *De Amicitia* recommends true friends to share possessions should adversity overtake one or the other.[19] The love-affair of Scogan is turned into a poetic equation for Scogan's friendship with Chaucer. Hence the half-concealed force of the concluding warning 'never eft Love defye'.[20] It may be suggested that the structure of the Letter to Scogan perhaps derives not from Horace's epistles or satires but from his Odes.[21]

Chaucer's achievement in the letter genre is stylistically distinct from that of his medieval forerunners and of his fifteenth- and sixteenth-century imitators. Only one English verse epistle[22] of Charles of Orleans aims at a conversational style. It is only moderately effective for it fails to achieve easy intimacy. Charles has not yet shed the time-worn amatory phraseology of the 'fine amour' mentality—or at least has not put it to sufficiently fresh use:[23]

> Offence? nay, þe offence hit is in me!
> For what, as loo, y ought me welle content
> In what ye say—so hit yowre plesere be:

18 Cf. W. H. French, 'The Meaning of Chaucer's *Envoy to Scogan*', *PMLA*, xxviii, 1913. pp. 289–92.

19 Cf. Jean de Meung's paraphrase of Cicero, in the English version, *Romaunt*, 5513 ff.

20 Cf. Cicero, *De Amicitia*, viii. 26 ff. where he links Love and Friendship etymologically: 'Amor enim, ex quo amicitia nominatur est . . .'; and xvii. 100 *passim*.

21 Cf. *Odes*, II.5; IV.12 for good examples of indirection as a structural device.

22 R. R. Steele, *The English Poems of Charles of Orleans, E.E.T.S.* (London, 1941), pp. 206–7.

23 Cf. Wyatt's more original handling of conventional phrases in 'Greting to you bothe yn hertye wyse' (K. Muir, *Collected Poems of Sir Thomas Wyatt* [London, 1949], pp. 139–40).

The which þe amverse took in myn entent.
I, crewelle, lo, and ye to pacient
Me to rebewke as of my gret outrage
And squaring of my ruggid fowle langage!

In the *Envoi a Scogan* the command of urbane conversational syntax and style, of sly and playful use of mythology, of structural indirection, together with the Horatian borrowing, marks Chaucer out as the first English poet to master the essentials of the Augustan verse epistle.

10

The Formulaic Theory and its Application to English Alliterative Poetry

PART OF THE PURPOSE of this book is to help give shape to the growing awareness that the linguistic and critical techniques applied to literature should be brought into closer relationship. This purpose takes many forms in the different chapters. The concern of this essay is with the analysis of the language of certain types of poetry into formulas—an area of linguistic study which has had much impact in recent years on the literary appreciation of important bodies of classical and medieval poetry. Here, the question of literary value has had to be asked again, and asked for the first time in the form: 'what kinds of excellence are possible in an art built on formulas?'[1]

A method of analysing poetic language which is causing us quite extensively to reappraise the aesthetic value of certain kinds of literature is obviously one whose terms and underlying assumptions should be thoroughly examined. It is the purpose of this essay first to make a critical survey of the origins of the formulaic theory, and then to discuss some of the chief developments and problems resulting from the application of the theory to Old and Middle English alliterative verse.

I

The formulaic approach to literature is perhaps best known to classicists. It was on the language of the Homeric poems that the

[1] An adaptation of a question in R. P. Creed 'On the possibility of criticizing Old English Poetry', *Texas Studies in Literature and Language*, iii (1961–2), p. 98.

key researches were made by a Harvard scholar, Milman Parry, 'whose name,' according to one critic, 'marks the second great turning point in modern Homeric scholarship'.[2] In the pioneer work of Parry those elements of Homer's diction which before had variously and inconclusively been termed epic cliché, stock epithet, etc., were convincingly explained as parts of a vast interlocking network of conventional formulas, whose semantic range covered everything the poet had to say and whose rhythm and form were such that they could be fitted rapidly and unerringly into both the sentence and metrical structure of the Greek hexameter line. Parry defined the formula as 'a group of words which is regularly employed under the same metrical conditions to express a given essential idea'.[3] Most formulas, he believed, could be grouped into systems where the formulas though not identical with each other had the same metrical value and sufficiently resembled each other in thought and words to be known to the poet as formulas of the same type ('Studies in the Epic Technique' I, pp. 85, 133; II, pp. 6 ff.). The formula was thus not a simple phrasal repetition:[4] it was capable of variation within a system and was intimately related to a specific portion of the Greek hexameter. In this identity with a recognized metrical unit lies the 'usefulness' of any particular formula—useful because the worker in the formulaic tradition knew unhesitatingly that at a certain point in the line the formula would ring metrically

[2] Cedric H. Whitman, *Homer and the Heroic Tradition* (Harvard, 1958), p. 4. Parry's ideas are most fully set out in: *L'épithète traditionnelle dans Homère* (Paris, 1928), where he demonstrates that the traditional epithet had little bearing on the meaning of the sentence and was employed to make nouns into phrases of the required metrical value and so to help the poet set the tale to hexameters; and 'Studies in the Epic Technique of Oral Verse-making. I: Homer and Homeric Style', *HSCP*, xli (1930), pp. 73–147, 'II: The Homeric Language as the Language of an Oral Poetry', *HSCP*, xliii (1932), pp. 1–50. For a full bibliography of Parry's writings see A. B. Lord 'Homer, Parry, and Huso', *American Journal of Archaeology*, lii (1948), pp. 43–4. Parry was, of course, far from being the first to notice the existence of poetry composed of repeated phrases but he was the pioneer in giving to such phenomena a consistent and convincing explanation.

[3] 'Studies in the Epic Technique. I', p. 80. See also II, pp. 6 f. As well as the formula, the concept of the 'theme' is connected with what has come to be known as the 'oral theory'. Discussion of the theme is not given here as emphasis is on the linguistic consequences of oral poesis. But see A. B. Lord, *The Singer of Tales* (Havard, 1960), ch. 4.

[4] Parry carefully distinguishes between true formulas which are the indispensable elements in making verse and repeated phrases used for literary effect and not related to a specific metrical unit (I, pp. 81–3, 122, 124).

true and also fit in syntactically with the typical patterns of the formulas lying on either side of it. Formulas, Parry shows, are so useful that they would relieve the poet of the time-consuming exercise of selection, for at any single moment there is usually only one group of words in the whole of the poetic language that will suffice and this group of words or formula is used to the exclusion of all others every time the same combination of metrical position, grammar, and sense appears. The system of formulas to which any particular formula belongs thus has the property of 'thrift' or 'economy', for no matter how large the system may be, no (or very little) duplication of function occurs (I, pp. 86, 87, 89). A system of formulas—and hence the whole poetic language, the sum of all formulaic systems—is comprehensive but rarely wastes its resources in casual variation.

Such a language, Parry argued, could only be a traditional medium: no man could have created by himself something so complex, so adaptable, so minutely designed for the easy expression of certain ideas in verse form; 'it must be the work of many poets over many generations' (II, p. 7; cf. I, pp. 184-5). If in form traditional, in function this poetic language with its enormous stock of ready-made parts seemed to be designed to facilitate sustained composition of hexameter lines at a speed necessary only in oral improvisation.[5] This is to say that the Homeric language provided a comprehensive system of techniques whereby a non-literate bard could swiftly compose and recite at one and the same time before an audience. The Homeric poems were in fact essentially oral poems.

To find support for this view, Parry, aided by his co-worker, A. B. Lord, collected recordings and texts of the oral poetry still surviving in part of Yugoslavia[6] to discover whether it had any of the linguistic features observed in Homer. Parry died before

[5] I, p. 138. Apart from schematization, other facts suggested an oral tradition: the great age of parts of the diction (I, pp. 135–7; cf. his 'The Homeric Gloss', *TAPA*, lix (1928), pp. 233–47); and the 'fairly large number of cases where the pure sound of one expression has suggested another which is altogether unlike it in meaning' (I, pp. 140–3).

[6] M. Murko, *La poésie populaire épique en Yougoslavie au début du xxe siècle* (Paris, 1929), pp. 16, 18, etc., had already indicated that oral poetry current in that region was based on repeated formulas.

full comparison could be made,[7] but Lord continued the work and has shown that Parry was substantially correct in seeing a parallel between Homer and this oral poetry. The mature findings of the jointly undertaken research are presented in Lord's book *The Singer of Tales*.[8] Here, however, as a result of the comparison with a living tradition, Lord shifts some of Parry's original emphasis. What had disturbed many admirers of the ancient Greek epics was the rigid functionalism of the formulaic style as Parry had revealed it, a functionalism that exhibited the relationship between metre and language virtually as one of cause and effect.[9] But Lord describes the pre-literate poetic medium as a language in its own right, assimilated slowly and naturally by ear during the poet's formative years: 'In studying the patterns and systems of oral narrative verse we are in reality observing the "grammar" of the poetry, a grammar superimposed, as it were, on the grammar of the language concerned. Or to alter the image, we find a special grammar within the grammar of the language, necessitated by the versification. . . . The speaker of this language, once he has mastered it, does not move any more mechanically within it than we do in ordinary speech. . . . He does not "memorize" formulas any more than we as children "memorize" language' (*The Singer of Tales*, pp. 35–6). What the would-be singer must acquire is the basic patterns behind the formulaic systems: 'the really significant element . . . is the setting up of various patterns that make adjustment of phrase and creation of phrases by analogy possible. This will be the whole basis of his art.'[10] The

[7] But see his article 'Whole Formulaic Verses in Greek and Southslavic Heroic Song', *TAPA*, lxiv (1933), pp. 179–97.

[8] A. B. Lord, *The Singer of Tales* (Harvard, 1960). See his earlier work: 'Homer and Huso. I: The Singer's Rests in Greek and Southslavic Heroic Song', *TAPA*, lxvii (1936), pp. 106–13; 'II: Narrative Inconsistencies in Homer and Oral Poetry', *TAPA*, lxix (1938), pp. 439–45.

[9] See, for example, *L'épithète traditionnelle*, p. 10: (the Homeric diction) 'en tant qu'elle est composée de formules, est due tout entière à l'influence du vers . . .'; and 'Studies in the Epic Technique. I', p. 138: 'in treating of the oral nature of the Homeric style we shall see that the question of a remnant of individuality in Homeric style disappears altogether'.

[10] *The Singer of Tales*, p. 37. For a similar defence of the Homeric language see Cedric H. Whitman, op. cit., pp. 13, 110 ff. Efforts of a different sort have been made to mitigate the metrical utilitarianism of the formula. George M. Calhoun 'The Art of Formula in Homer', *Classical Philology*, xxx (1935), pp. 215–27, attempted to show that lines introducing speeches were not so mechanical in use as Parry had implied ('Whole Formulaic

singer, then, has a 'second language', parallel to his spoken one but significantly different from it in that it has the added dimension of metre. Metre in this other language is almost an aspect of grammar: phrases do not 'make sense' unless they have a certain rhythmical pattern. The basic element of this language is therefore not the word but the phrasal pattern of a grammatical and metrical value, a 'grammetrical' unit.[11]

As the results of Parry's work began to affect other areas of literary research, further modifications had to be made to the theory and definition of the formula which their originator had implied were generally applicable to formulaic poetry.[12] James Ross, in a study of the oral lyrics of the Western Isles of Scotland,[13] found that he had to introduce the notion of 'conceptual formulas', recurrent ideas whose 'variety' of 'expressions shows that what makes an idea useful to the poet is not its availability in a fixed verbal form or in a system of metrically similar statements' (p. 4). Ross also raises an important logical objection to the criterion of metrical utility used by Parry in all his explanations of oral linguistic form. This, argues Ross, is to presuppose what is impossible, namely, 'The existence of a given metrical form prior to and during the evolution of the poetic language' (p. 5, fn. 19).

[11] P. J. Wexler's term (see above, ch. 6, p. 104) seems peculiarly appropriate for describing the dual character of the linguistic units of which an oral poetic language seems to be composed. It must be added that the conditions in Middle English alliterative verse that make a joint categorization in terms of these two linguistic dimensions helpful are not the same as those discussed by Wexler.

[12] See, for example, J. Rychner, *La Chanson de geste: essai sur l'art épique des jongleurs* (Geneva and Lille, 1955); C. M. Bowra, *Heroic Poetry* (London, 1952), which refers to the oral poetry of, among others, the Yugoslavs, Russians, modern Greeks, Albanians, and Asiatic Tatars; W. Whallon, 'Formulaic Poetry in the Old Testament', *Comparative Literature*, xv (1963), pp. 1–14.

[13] James Ross, 'Formulaic Composition in Gaelic Oral Poetry,' *MP*, lvii (1959–60), pp. 1–12.

Verses in Greek and Southslavic Heroic Song') and that they frequently varied because of the association of a certain type with a certain attitude or mood of the speaker. It might also be added (*pace* Lord p. 30 and fn. 3, p. 282) that formula in so far as it is repetition is necessary or delightful to unsophisticated audiences for other than metrical reasons. C. M. Bowra, *Heroic Poetry* (London, 1952), pp. 226, 231, thinks that the formula is helpful to such listeners because it eases the burden of comprehension for them and satisfies an innate desire for the familiar. Melville Jacobs, *The Content and Style of an Oral Literature* (Chicago, 1959), pp. 220–50, records a number of stylized and repetitive expressions from the non-metrical tales and myths in the Clackamas dialect of Chinook.

Ross adds little more, but one may suppose that somehow metre and formula originally developed together, the play of analogy slowly making ever more numerous those patterns which seemed to represent the rhythmical norm and eradicating those that were less common, until the point was reached where what the modern mind perceives as metre was established. In making this logical objection Ross perhaps overlooks the fact that an oral poetic language (like any language) continues to evolve and was not created—even lengthily—once for all. In this continuing development, one of the operative factors would be the metre (whether consciously recognized or not) which would govern the shape of new phrases and preserve archaic but metrically indispensable forms.[14] The objection may be useful, however, in deterring scholars from erecting metre as an external standard for the oral poet or from regarding it as something 'hard' that the singer had difficulty in coping with. The linguistic forms for coping easily and rapidly with the metre were always available simply because it was only in the range of formulas employed by a tradition that the metre could be said to exist at all.

II

The application of Parry's work to Old and Middle English literature had a considerable impact on work in these fields. F. P. Magoun initiated the introduction of the methods used on Homer and Slavic poetry with analyses of Cædmon's *Hymn* and a section of *Beowulf*.[15] From these he concluded that the greater part of

[14] For the preservation of metrically useful forms, see the references in fn. 5 above to the great age of parts of the Homeric diction. Pressure of rhythm, Parry thinks, also leads to the creation of artificial forms ('Studies in the Epic Technique. II', pp. 19, 33–5), and largely accounts for the mixed dialect of the poems, Ionic forms being used in later stages of development in the traditional style, only where they do not disturb the rhythmic patterns of older Aeolic formulas (II, pp. 37, 45, 47). A characteristic feature of diction noticed by A. Brink, *Stab und Wort im Gawain* (Halle, 1920), in *Sir Gawain and the Green Knight*, and other fourteenth-century alliterative poems may be a special form of the preservation of older words and phrases for metrical utility. Brink shows that among groups of synonyms it was almost invariably the archaic words that appeared in alliteration while more recently acquired synonyms filled the final, non-alliterating stave.

[15] F. P. Magoun, Jr., 'Oral-Formulaic Character of Anglo-Saxon Narrative Poetry', *Speculum*, xxviii (1953), pp. 446–65. See also his 'Bede's story of Cædman: The Case History of an Anglo-Saxon Oral Singer', *Speculum*, xxx (1955), pp. 49–63.

Old English narrative verse was formulaic and therefore of an oral character; that before being set down in script it was first composed in a manner indistinguishable from that used by singers who drew on a traditional linguistic stock to improvise verse before an audience, a manner perhaps exemplified by the *scop* who extolled the achievements of Beowulf in extempore narrative on the ride back from the mere of monsters.

Magoun makes this inference from his analyses, despite the fact that for several centuries since the introduction of Christianity poets had writing available as an apparently superior method of composing poetry, because, as he says, 'the recurrence in a given poem of an appreciable number of formulas or formulaic phrases brands the latter as oral, just as a lack of such repetitions marks a poem as composed in a lettered tradition'.[16] The actual existence in Anglo-Saxon England of such a lettered tradition does not necessarily militate against Magoun's opinion on the essentially oral character of Old English poetry. Mere knowledge of writing is no testimony to its use for poetry.[17] Writing was too laborious and expensive a craft to be exploited on a large scale for popular entertainment; and oral poets had little need for permanent texts, their ancient methods being perfectly adequate as long as the poetry demanded was of the traditional kind. The appearance in manuscript of some Old English poetry may well be the exception rather than the rule and doubtless had behind it a relatively untouched native oral tradition.

Students of Old English who have written on the formulaic character of the poetry since Magoun have been less confident about the rigid dichotomy he makes between the oral style and the written, and it is on this point that much subsequent debate has turned. Most scholars have been able to support Magoun

[16] 'Oral-Formulaic Character of Anglo-Saxon Narrative Poetry', pp. 446–7.

[17] For the relationship between literature and writing in early times see H. M. and N. K. Chadwick, *The Growth of Literature* (Cambridge, 1932), i, pp. 5 and 475 ff. For some purposes, often connected with religion and ritual, there may even have been positive resistance to writing in some primitive societies; see J. A. Notopoulos 'Mnemosyne in Oral Literature', *TAPA*, lxix (1938), pp. 475 ff. As far as the question of the oral nature of the Homeric texts is concerned Parry asserts that the existence or not of writing at the time when the poems were first composed is quite irrelevant ('Studies in the Epic Technique. I', p. 79, fn. 1).

unreservedly in his assertion that Old English poetry was largely made up of traditional compositional elements, but his interpretation of this fact to explain the genesis of the poems has been received with less favour. Some objectors have suggested that perhaps literate poets could work—would find it extremely advantageous to work—with the formulaic language; others that some poems were too 'artistic' or too learned for what they conceived to be the necessarily crude methods of pre-literate versifiers. But artistic excellence by itself need argue no more conclusively against oral poesis than does the availability of writing. How can the twentieth-century scholar presume to have instinctive knowledge of what excellence is or is not appropriate to early oral poetry? It may be that a popular theme, or poem of several related themes, as it is progressively developed and refined by a succession of oral poets, could achieve a perfection of form and a density of utterance perhaps even beyond the capacity of written literature. Yet in many minds formulaic poetry is *a priori* equated with the imperfect and fragmentary, and thought inimical to the creation of literature of value. Fairly typical is the misconception voiced by R. W. V. Elliot. On the subject of *Beowulf* he remarks that 'no amount of fashionable emphasis upon the "oral-formulaic" nature of Old English poetry can explain such art away'.[18] This misrepresents the situation because students of formulaic techniques have not been concerned to 'explain away' anything but simply to draw attention to a vital factor in the composition of much early poetry in order that its real merit may emerge more clearly. Their contention has not been that artistic merit and formulaic composition are mutually exclusive concepts, but that the artistic merit is of a fundamentally different order from that to be expected from written literature. Nevertheless, Elliot is not alone in suggesting that the criterion of artistic merit may be used to eliminate the possibility of oral composition in some Old English poems. R. D. Stevick thinks the detailed art-form of the *Wife's Lament* is incompatible with oral extemporization; and Kemp Malone in a review voices

[18] 'Landscape and Rhetoric in the Middle-English Alliterative Poetry', *Melbourne Critical Review*, iv (1961), pp. 65–76.

plainly his opinion that 'the *Beowulf* poet was no minstrel, strumming a harp and composing verse as he strummed [but] a sophisticated literary artist, who gave careful thought to what he was doing ...'.[19] C. M. Bowra likewise considers it impossible for the Homeric poems to have been improvised because of their artistry (*Heroic Poetry*, p. 240), though in the case of these poems J. A. Notopoulos, adding to what Parry discovered about the details of language, has been able to explain the larger techniques of organization—foreshadowing, retrospection, ring-composition—entirely in terms of the practical role these play in a poetry which must be essentially oral.[20]

The alleged incongruity between artistic merit and oral creation is not, however, the only form of argument brought forward in an effort to make some sort of compromise between the learned and primitive method of making poetry, a compromise generally felt necessary for the conditions known to have prevailed in Anglo-Saxon England. Claes Schaar finds it inconceivable that 'the incomparable advantage of employing the ready-made elaborate means of expressing a variety of current ideas'[21] would be put aside when writing came in favour of devising new poetic methods. He goes on to point out a logical fallacy in Magoun's argument (and by implication in Parry's on Homer) which rested on the false reasoning that if oral poetry was formulaic then formulaic poetry was oral. Oral poetry could be shown empirically to be formulaic, but if the situation were turned round, what conclusions could legitimately be drawn from a style based on formulas? The historical truth would probably have to include a transitional period during which primitive and learned methods were used together. He points in illustration to the poems of Cynewulf where formulas are found in conjunction with learned allusions (p. 303).

But Lord, while recognizing a transitional period of another

[19] Respectively: 'The Oral-Formulaic Analyses of Old English Verse', *Speculum*, xxxvii (1962), p. 387, fn. 12; *ES*, xli (1960), p. 5—briefly and approvingly referred to by A. Bonjour, 'A Post-Script on *Beowulf* and the Singer Theory', *Twelve Beowulf Papers* (Neuchatel, 1962).

[20] 'Continuity and Interconnection in Homeric Oral Composition,' *TAPA*, lxxxii (1951), pp. 81–101.

[21] 'On a New Theory of Old English Poetic Diction,' *Neophilologus*, xl (1956), p. 302.

sort, strongly objects to any acceptance of a transitional text or style: 'The written technique is not compatible with the oral technique, and the two could not possibly combine to form another, a third, a transitional technique.'[22] The ambiguous fact of the appearance in writing of what he accepts as oral poems he attributes either to 'autograph oral' (where the oral poet having become literate dictates to himself) or to 'dictated oral' (where another person writes from the singer's dictation). The transitional period, as Lord sees it, is one of overlap not continuation: a period when oral and written methods exist side by side but with no substantial continuity from one to the other. There will be no transitional style because the old exponent of the oral technique does not usually become a writer and because the new lettered poet, apart from carrying over the odd traditional phrase, uses the methods of free composition which writing makes possible. Texts from the transitional period will belong to one or the other of the two easily distinguishable types. One cannot help thinking that Lord is wrong in this matter, or at least generalizing too freely from a single instance. The possibility should be recognized that different conditions may act differently on what appears to be a common cultural product. Lord's rigid distinction may well apply in Yugoslavia where oral poetry was competing with the printed text, other forms of entertainment, and the spread of literacy; it may not be so appropriate in classical or medieval times when oral poetry was competing with the manuscript, which often implied oral delivery if not improvisation. Often the manuscript carries a metrical form through from a period of oral to one of written transmission, as it seems to do in Anglo-Saxon times, to judge by the similarities between extant English alliterative verse and that of some Old Germanic languages, similarities doubtless acquired from a period before the migrations when the Germanic tribes may have shared a common oral poetry. In order to reconcile this continuation of a poetic type with Lord's rigid distinction between the two kinds of

[22] *The Singer of Tales*, p. 129. He expresses the view at length in ch. 6, 'Writing and Oral Tradition', pp. 124–38. The categorical distinction made by Magoun and Lord between oral and written literature follows Parry's: 'Whole Formulaic Verses in Greek and Southslavic Heroic Song', p. 180.

literature one would have to suppose that an oral poetry consisted of an empty metrical form which immediately writing was employed could be filled out in ways quite unconnected with the rich store of inherited formulas and verse techniques. This appears untrue at least of Homer. Parry observes that most metrical 'irregularities' result either from a change within a formula or from the grouping of certain formulas (I, pp. 138–9; cf. Magoun, pp. 458–9); an observation which leads one to suggest that the actual units of the linguistic material have a greater pull on the singer's or poet's rendering than any abstract metrical system. Further, as Lord himself describes earlier, the oral poetic method which he witnessed among the Yugoslavs is virtually a second language assimilated by the young singer in solid form by way of formulas and patterns (pp. 21, 32, 37, 41, 43, etc., also pp. 3–4 above); and the singer, quite unconscious of metre, 'when . . . pressed . . . to say what a line is, . . . will be entirely baffled by the question' (p. 25). An oral poetry would consist in its concrete, time-honoured elements and not in an abstract form capable of being filled out by different linguistic material in a process of free composition. Admittedly, the traditional style was engendered by the need for speedy composition and as soon as writing began to play a part this need vanished. But if demand for the same kind of entertainment continued then the vehicle for the entertainment would tend to be preserved as well. In the Middle Ages if not in twentieth-century Yugoslavia the same habits of mind would continue for a long time and the custom of oral delivery, the necessary means of publication for centuries after the advent of writing, would perpetuate a great part of the traditional methods, and allow the potential poets of the next generation to absorb them by ear in much the same way as in the past unlettered epoch. One can thus readily imagine that a written poetry based on the cultural assumptions of its parent oral poetry would long preserve the traditional metre and methods of the improvising art, before cultural change brought about new literary expectations and different means of composing poetry.

Schaar is not alone among Old English scholars in finding the concept 'transitional text' necessary despite the blunt repudiation of it by the original theorists. Versions of the formulaic theory modified to admit some element of writing have multiplied rapidly in recent years. R. E. Diamond thinks that written formulaic poetry is possible but that it is impossible from internal evidence alone to determine whether any given formulaic poem is oral or not.[23] But he demonstrates, by checking against the whole OE poetic corpus, that the signed poems of Cynewulf, often regarded as the work of a learned man, have a 62.7 per cent formulaic content (p. 234). W. Whallon finds quite acceptable the idea of a literate man learning and becoming familiar with oral poetry and its accepted aids and then being able to write his own compositions in like manner.[24] J. J. Campbell[25] thinks that the introduction of letters must have greatly influenced the native poetic tradition, but expresses a firm conviction that the traditional devices engendered by the oral situation 'could be, and were carried over into written literature' (p. 88). His analysis of *The Seafarer* suggests that if Magoun's strict separation of oral from literary style on the basis of formula density were applied, then this poem would be split into two distinct sections, for the first 38 lines are far more demonstrably formulaic than the rest. R. D. Stevick states unequivocally his opinion that 'the records we have are . . . more likely to be the work of English monks and churchmen rather than scops; they are educated in Christian Latin literature, and were in practice carrying over oral traditions into lettered poetry, not merely transcribing performances of oral singers'.[26]

One scholar of formulaic method in Old English poetry who stands notably apart from reinterpretations that assume a dependence on writing is R. P. Creed. Together with other scholars he provides evidence for the formulaic basis of style of OE poetry —from an ingeniously fresh angle in 'The Making of an Anglo-Saxon Poem',[27] where he attempts to re-enact the creative process

[23] 'The Diction of the Signed Poems of Cynewulf', *PQ*, xxxviii (1959), pp. 228–41.

[24] 'The Diction of *Beowulf*', *PMLA*, lxxvi (1961), pp. 309–19.

[25] 'Oral Poetry in *The Seafarer*', *Speculum*, xxxv (1960), pp. 87–96. See also W. A. O'Neil 'Another Look at Oral Poetry in *The Seafarer*', ibid., pp. 595–600.

[26] 'The Oral-Formulaic Analyses of Old English Verse', p. 383.

[27] *ELH*, xxvi (1959), pp. 445–54. It might well be objected that by this method Creed proves possible the opposite of what he believes. If he can effectively use the oral techniques

in our earliest poetry by taking to pieces four lines of *Beowulf* and remaking them according to the original sense with the aid of alternative formulas. Creed has made a systematic study of the language of *Beowulf* in an unpublished doctoral thesis from which he provides facts and figures to support the view expressed in his article that 'The diction of *Beowulf* is schematized to an extraordinary degree'. Illustrating this schematization Creed says that 'roughly every fifth verse' and 'an essential part of every second verse' are 'repeated elsewhere in the poem' (p. 445). He differs from the majority of OE scholars in concluding from such evidence that the maker of the poem is employing the genuine oral method—is a 'singer' who 'composes rapidly'.[28] In a later article tackling the difficult task of constructing a more relevant mode of literary appreciation for formulaic poems, he admits the possibility that *Beowulf* may not be the record of an actual performance but still insists that the singer (not poet) was indubitably trained in oral techniques.[29]

A direct extension of the application of Parry's methods to Old English has been the start of a similar application to Middle English alliterative poetry.[30] The introduction of the method to Middle English studies was made by R. A. Waldron in an unpublished thesis and subsequently in an article in *Speculum*.[31]

[28] P. 446. Creed expresses the same opinion in 'The *Andswarode*-System in Old English Poetry', *Speculum*, xxxii (1957), pp. 523–8.

[29] 'On the Possibility of Criticizing Old English Poetry', *Texas Studies in Literature and Language*, iii (1961–2), pp. 97–106.

[30] The article by A. C. Baugh, 'Improvisation in the Middle English Romances', *Procs. of the American Philosophic Society*, ciii (1959), pp. 418–54, although concerned with metrical rather than alliterative romances, is important because it shows that formulaic composition of verse in Middle English is by no means restricted to the alliterative tradition.

[31] *The Diction of English Alliterative Romances*, M. A. Thesis (London, 1953)—Waldron was familiar with Magoun's work in Old English from the latter's lectures at London University in January, 1952; 'Oral-Formulaic Technique and Middle English Alliterative Poetry', *Speculum*, xxxii (1957), pp. 792–804.

---

in the privacy of his study, then how much more effectively might the Anglo-Saxon monk have done like-wise? The use of alternative formulas also inadvertently demonstrates the lack in the Old English poetic medium of 'thrift' (revealed also by comparison with Homer, W. Whallon, art. cit., pp. 311–19), a quality Parry thought essential to the oral style. But see Lord's more liberal interpretation of 'thrift' in oral poetic language, op. cit., pp. 50–3.

Waldron's original work was concerned principally with formulas that fill the metrical portion between the caesura and the end of the long alliterative line. The formulas involved were not exact repetitions. Waldron's interest lay in those second half lines which characteristically ended on one of a limited number of words (e.g. *askes*, *out of lyfe*, *lastez*, *herte*, *wordes*, *dedes*, etc.), and the thesis presents the results of combing sixteen alliterative romances for a certain number of these second half-line formulas. The single element of likeness among all the phrases in any list is the final word (or words), but each list can usually be broken down into several systems of phrases having more in common than just the final word. The conclusion Waldron thinks should be drawn from these long lists which cater for many of the poet's needs is certainly not that the poems are orally composed—'the plain fact of Latin and French originals makes a theory of oral composition for these particular poems (or for some of them at least) quite untenable'.[32] The intention is 'to show a tradition of oral composition *behind* the ME alliterative romances', and thus 'to throw some new light . . . on the sudden reappearance of alliterative metre in the fourteenth century after a gap of three centuries'.[33] In his article Waldron puts the emphasis on the prosodic utility of the conventional elements and on their easy adaptability to different contexts; and so suggests that they are not mere relics preserved in the amber of a purely written literature but still living parts of a language—albeit diminishing—once made necessary by the exigencies of oral improvisation and still indispensable for the continuation of a long-familiar poetry demanded by audience and reader alike.

Further, Waldron shows that analogy, which is the basis of all formulaic language, can lie at a level deeper than the merely superficial similarity of identical wording by introducing his concept of the 'rhythmical-syntactical mould'. By this concept

[32] Thesis, p. 19; cf. art. cit., p. 792. The fact that in the Middle English alliterative poems we have a high degree of formulaic composition—granted that Waldron proves this—coupled with close translation from literary sources (e.g. *The Destruction of Troy* and *The Wars of Alexander*) is one that may well have a bearing on the question of formulaic texts in other fields.

[33] Art. cit., p. 794.

he formulates what appears to be a special case in Middle English alliterative verse of a grammetrical unit, for the mould consists of a metrically unchanging grammatical construction which, for purposes of explanation, is said to be 'filled in' with lexical items suited to context or alliteration (art. cit., p. 798 and fn. 14). There is usually a verbal constant here in the unstressed, 'grammatical' words of the half-line; this part forms a framework with slots, as it were, into which the important, and usually alliterating, words can be readily dropped. The example of a mould that Waldron uses for illustration is:

× × / × × (×) / (×)
I shall . . . thee (you) . . . .

This is a first half-line grammatical formula where the first space is 'filled' by a verb and the second by its direct object. Some realizations are: *Wars of Alexander* 3735 *I sal declare ȝow þe cas*; *Cleanness* 802 *I schal fette yow a fatte*; *Destruction of Troy* 7985 *I shall fast the þis forward*; *Gawain* 2251 *I schall gruch þe no grwe.*[34] Devices such as these, like those very similar half-line formulaic systems in Old English discussed by Magoun—*on x-dagum, on (ofer, geond) x-rade, þæt wæs x cyning, etc.* (pp. 450–52), make for easy reconciliation of two very different sorts of formal requirement: the rhythmical and the alliterative.

To how great an extent Middle English alliterative verse can be dependent on formulas and formulaic phrases Waldron shows by means of a sample analysis from *Morte Arthur* (and from *Gawain* as well in the thesis) after the manner used by Parry, Lord and Magoun (pp. 802–4). From this analysis it appears that in the first twenty-five lines of the poem only two have no part repeated elsewhere in the sixteen poems, and the 'supporting evidence', recording the other instances of the formulas, reveals that the poet was drawing on a body of poetic techniques widespread in use and traditional in origin. Many of the formulas

[34] Examples of other types of mould given are: *as soon as the* (NOUN) (VERB); *be the* (NOUN) *never so* (ADJ.) followed by main clause filling second half-line; *the first* (NOUN) *that he* (VERB). The unstressed verbal constant is not always present; some formulaic patterns are purely grammatical. One example (p. 799) 'contains three stresses and consists of an imperative verb, plus a noun meaning "man" in the vocative, plus a prepositional phrase: *Parl. Three Ages* 193 "*And wonne, wy, in thi witt, . . .*"; *Wars Alex.* 1990 "*Fyne, fole, of þi fare . . .*", etc.'

recorded by Waldron had been noted before and often slightingly written off as 'tags' or taken as signs of single authorship, but Waldron's adaption of the Parry-Lord theory produces a more systematic and satisfying explanation, one that is more likely to furnish the evidence for the often discussed but hitherto meagrely demonstrated notion of an oral continuity between Old and Middle English alliterative poetry.

One type of formula, however, thought by Waldron to be part of the oral style, has been questioned. The existence of the rhythmical-syntactical mould, a formulaic system whose component formulas are related one to the other not by verbal but by grammatical likeness, has been disputed in a recent article by J. Finlayson.[35] This writer asserts that the structural likenesses observed by Waldron between metrically similar phrases are 'simply the commonplaces of grammatical structure' and that 'to speak about a syntactical-grammatical structure as the mould into which meaning can be poured is to say no more than that the English language has a discernible syntactical structure. . . . All language is in this sense a formula' (p. 375). What Finlayson seems to be saying is that one would expect to find certain grammatical units invariably occupying certain metrical spans in the natural course of a poet's *ad hoc* adaption of his linguistic resources to his metrical specification, and that the poet has no specially rapid means of selecting at any given moment from the total possible constructions at his command. But such an argument assumes that users of the traditional verse conceived ideas without poetic form and that they had a sophisticated notion of metre to whose demands they could trim their unformed linguistic material. The linguistic features of the poetry suggest that such was not the case. The elaborate and extensive workings of analogy at all levels, and more especially the consistent relationship of certain constructions with certain segments of the alliterative line, suggest that grammar and metre were not resolved by the poet moment by moment, half-line to half-line, but that there pre-existed in his mind basic patterns which were grammetrical, which in a long-standing poetic language were the

[35] 'Formulaic Technique in *Morte Arthure*', *Anglia*, lxxxi (1963), pp. 372–93.

counterparts to normal linguistic systems. These patterns were traditionally shaped and as much 'known' to the exponent of the art as any of his more obvious techniques.

Finlayson seems to recognize that the alliterative style was originally created by the pressures of oral improvisation. From first-hand experience of this art in Yugoslavia, Lord concludes that it is the inexperienced singer who relies on verbally fixed phrases, and that the better or more experienced singer tends more and more to create new phrases on the pattern of those impressed on his mind when young.[36] Finlayson is led to underestimate the usefulness of such sub-semantic patterns to the worker in a traditional verse-medium—whether oral or written—because he ignores the implications of metre. It is a question of discovering not that the language of alliterative poetry has 'a discernible syntactical structure' but that this structure is composed of grammatical units which are co-extensive with metrical units and which exist as such in the poet's mind. In practice, the principle of grammatical analogy can be seen at work in the Middle English poems, as even the few illustrations cited here will suggest; and a grammatical matrix is the ultimate shaping force behind many a common expression. One need only refer to the second half-line type *ADJ./ADV. plus INFIN.*, a construction almost unknown in the first half-line but common in the second, and so numerous in expressions of the type *grym to behold* that these are recorded by Oakden as 'tags'.[37]

The question of whether phrases related to each other by an unvarying metrical and grammatical form are to be accounted a part of the formulaic technique is only one of a number which the application of oral-formulaic analysis to English literature has raised, and doubtless will continue to raise. Some of the fresh problems have been touched on here; the solutions to these—if within our grasp—will make clear much that is of vital im-

[36] *The Singer of Tales*, pp. 36, 37, 42, 43, etc. Parry also seems to find groups of phrases in Homer related by similarity of construction (e.g. 'Studies in the Epic Technique. I', p. 133). W. A. O'Neil, art. cit., emphasizes the importance of formulaic syntactic patterns in Old English poetry. For a demonstration of the metrical and syntactic unity of phrases in *Beowulf* see Lord's analysis of ll. 1473–87 (p. 199) and the relevant notes (pp. 297–301).

[37] J. P. Oakden, *Alliterative Poetry in Middle English*, vol. ii, (Manchester, 1935), p. 382.

portance for understanding the real nature and history of early English poetry. Of all problems, perhaps the most difficult and ultimately the most important is the one alluded to in the first paragraph: that of the literary value of poems composed largely or entirely of formulas. There are two dangers here: one is to ignore the implications of the formulaic content and cling to conventional critical approaches; the other is to make the facts of the formulaic style into the basis of a despairing attitude that views many older poems as quasi-mechanical exercises that could not possibly have interest or value for the serious student of literature. A true appreciation of such poetry must be built on the fact that in their different degrees the *Odyssey* and *Beowulf* and *Sir Gawain and the Green Knight* are simultaneously formulaic and great works of art.

Index

Index

Index